FOUL DEEDS & SUSPICI
IN READING

TRUE CRIME FROM WHARNCLIFFE

Foul Deeds and Suspicious Deaths Series

Barking, Dagenham & Chadwell Heath
Barnsley
Bath
Bedford
Birmingham
More Foul Deeds Birmingham
Black Country
Blackburn and Hyndburn
Bolton
Bradford
Brighton
Bristol
Cambridge
Carlisle
Chesterfield
Cumbria
More Foul Deeds Chesterfield
Colchester
Coventry
Croydon
Derby
Durham
Ealing
Fens
Folkstone and Dover
Grimsby
Guernsey
Guildford
Halifax
Hampstead, Holborn and St Pancras

Huddersfield
Hull
Jersey
Leeds
Leicester
Lewisham and Deptford
Liverpool
London's East End
London's West End
Manchester
Mansfield
More Foul Deeds Wakefield
Newcastle
Newport
Norfolk
Northampton
Nottingham
Oxfordshire
Pontefract and Castleford
Portsmouth
Rotherham
Scunthorpe
Southend-on-Sea
Southport
Staffordshire and the Potteries
Stratford and South Warwickshire
Tees
Warwickshire
Wigan
York

OTHER TRUE CRIME BOOKS FROM WHARNCLIFFE

A-Z of London Murders
A-Z of Yorkshire Murders
Black Barnsley
Brighton Crime and Vice 1800-2000
Durham Executions
Essex Murders
Executions & Hangings in Newcastle
  and Morpeth
Norfolk Mayhem and Murder

Norwich Murders
Strangeways Hanged
Unsolved Murders in Victorian &
  Edwardian London
Unsolved Norfolk Murders
Unsolved Yorkshire Murders
Warwickshire's Murderous Women
Yorkshire Hangmen
Yorkshire's Murderous Women

Please contact us via any of the methods below for more information
or a catalogue
WHARNCLIFFE BOOKS
47 Church Street, Barnsley, South Yorkshire, S70 2AS
Tel: 01226 734555 • 734222 • Fax: 01226 734438
email: enquiries@pen-and-sword.co.uk
website: www.wharncliffebooks.co.uk

Foul Deeds & Suspicious Deaths in
READING

John J Eddleston

Wharncliffe Books

First Published in Great Britain in 2009 by
Wharncliffe Books
an imprint of
Pen and Sword Books Limited,
47 Church Street, Barnsley,
South Yorkshire. S70 2AS

ISBN: 978 1 84563 113 0

A CIP catalogue record of this book is available from the
British Library.

Printed in the United Kingdom by
the MPG Books Group

Pen & Sword Books Ltd incorporates the imprints of
Pen & Sword Aviation, Pen & Sword Maritime, Pen & Sword Military,
Wharncliffe Local History, Pen & Sword Select, Pen & Sword Military Classics,
Leo Cooper, Remember When, Seaforth Publishing and Frontline Publishing.

For a complete list of Pen & Sword titles please contact:
PEN & SWORD BOOKS LIMITED
47 Church Street, Barnsley, South Yorkshire, S70 2AS, England.
E-mail: enquiries@pen-and-sword.co.uk
Website: www.pen-and-sword.co.uk

Contents

Introduction

The city of Reading, and the surrounding areas, hold some fascinating stories of murder.

The early chapters of this book carry a theme of women, driven to distraction by unwanted pregnancies, who, at their wit's ends, deposited their offspring into the cold waters of one of the rivers flowing through the area. The exception, of course, was Amelia Dyer, the infamous Reading baby-farmer, who turned this practice into a lucrative business. We will never know just how many innocent victims died at her hands.

There is, also, the still unsolved murder of Alfred Oliver, who was murdered in his tobacconist's shop; a crime for which an American actor suffered, in effect, a trial by coroner's inquisition.

There are those where the person found guilty of the crime suffered death by hanging. One of these was George Russell in 1948. Read his story for yourself and decide if he really was guilty of the crime which claimed his life.

Finally, there are the more modern murders including the red-mini murder and the gravel pits murders. There are even crimes which involved an Elvis Presley Fan Club, and religious sacrifice.

The foul deeds in this book involve murders over a period of more than one hundred years and show a darker side of parts of the county of Berkshire.

8

Acknowledgements

There are a number of people and organisations I would wish to thank for their valued assistance in the preparing of this book.

My deepest appreciation must go to Yvonne Eddleston, my wife. Not only did she help with the research, making copious notes on some of the cases, but she also proofread every chapter. Her efforts only served to make this work better.

I must also thank the staff of The National Archives at Kew. It is always a pleasure to work there and the staff are amongst the most helpful I have encountered. They also assisted with many of the illustrations within the book.

My thanks too must go to the staff of the British Library's newspaper archive at Colindale, north London, for producing many newspapers covering the later cases.

Finally, I would wish to offer my thanks to my publishers, Wharncliffe Books, and especially Mr Rupert Harding.

CHAPTER 1

An Unkind Man
Mary Newell
1858

Samuel Mortlake, the master of the Henley Union Workhouse, travelled up to Reading on business, on Wednesday 11 August 1858.

At one stage, Samuel's business took him past the local police station and he could not help but notice a small crowd gathered around a photograph, pasted up near the main door. Curiosity having got the better of Samuel, he too stopped to take a look at whatever seemed to be generating so much interest.

The photograph was of the body of a male baby, aged some three months or so, recovered from the river near King's Meadow the day before, 10 August. Whilst the rest of the small crowd gazed at the picture with idle curiosity, Samuel looked at it with something approaching horror, for he had recognised the child.

That evening, Samuel returned to the workhouse and made some further enquiries. These appeared to confirm his worst fears, so the next day, 12 August, he returned to Reading, called at the police station and asked to be allowed to view the body itself. Permission was granted and, finally, a positive identification was made. The body recovered from the river was that of Richard Newell.

The river at King's Meadow where Mary Newell put her child into the water.
The author

Samuel Mortlake went on to make a full statement to the police. In that statement he explained that on 11 January, twenty-two-year-old Mary Newell had been admitted to his workhouse. At the time, she was pregnant but refused to give any details as to who the father might be.

On 7 May, Mary gave birth to a healthy baby boy, who she named Richard. She then remained in the workhouse until 9 August, when she announced that she was leaving, to go to a friend's house. Mary was interviewed by Mr Mortlake before she left and said she had received a letter from a cousin, a Mrs Bakehouse, who had offered her a place for herself and the child. Mr Mortlake tried, once again, to discover something about the child's father, but Mary would give nothing away, apart from the fact that he lived in Reading. She had then left the workhouse, at some time between 1.00pm and 2.00pm.

Something of Mary's history was, of course, known to the workhouse authorities and they were able to give the police details of her family. It was this, which led Constable David Pitts to Mary's mother's house, at Ipsden. Mary was at the house and when Constable Pitts asked her where her child was, Mary replied that she had left it with a nurse, but was either unable, or unwilling, to say precisely where. Not satisfied with this answer, Pitts said that he would have to take Mary into custody whereupon she broke down and cried: 'I was forced to do it.'

Taken to Oxford police station, Mary Newell made a full written statement, admitting that she was responsible for her son's death. She explained that she had been in service at Wallingford since 1853 and had become rather friendly with a gentleman named Robert Francis, whom she had known for some six years in all. The relationship developed and, in due course, Mary found herself pregnant. By now it was close to Christmas and, naturally growing concerned as to what might happen to her, Mary had gone to Robert and explained her predicament. To her surprise, Robert had shown little interest in her welfare and had simply announced that he was unable to help her, as he was now keeping company with another woman. At her wit's end, Mary had left her job and gone to stay at the workhouse in Henley, some seven miles away. There she had given birth to Richard and, after a time, had decided to go back to Robert and again ask him for help.

Robert ran a shop in Friar Street, Reading and on 9 August, after she had left the workhouse, Mary had confronted him there. Far from showing the slightest interest in her or the child, Robert had, rather unkindly, simply walked out of the shop leaving Mary with his sister. Mary waited for him to return, but in due course, the sister said she had to put the shutters up for the night. Mary stood outside and then walked up and down Friar Street for some time. When it was clear that Robert was not going to return, she walked on and found herself at King's Meadow, near the river.

Unsure even what she was doing, Mary stripped her son down to his nappy, tied a small bag she carried around his waist, and weighted it with stones. She then watched as her son lay on his back on the riverbank, kicking his feet. Then, suddenly, he kicked once again and rolled over, into the river. She then walked to her mother's house where she stayed until her arrest.

Charged with murder, Mary Newell appeared before Mr Justice Erle on 20 December 1858. Mr Griffiths detailed the case for the prosecution whilst Mary was defended by Mr Cripps. Throughout the trial, Mary was constantly in an almost fainting condition and often had to be assisted by the officials set to guard her.

Charles Duffield explained to the court that on Tuesday 10 August, he had been cray-fishing in the King's Meadow, close to the mill, with a friend of his, Francis Shepherd. At the time, Duffield was standing on the riverbank whilst Shepherd was standing in the river, some two or three feet from the bank.

At one stage, Duffield saw a flash of something pale in the weeds close by. Thinking at first that it might be a fish, he glanced over and, as he gazed, the flash came again. To his horror he saw that it wasn't a fish, but appeared to be a small, human hand. He shouted across to Shepherd who waded over to where Duffield indicated and grabbed the hand. Shepherd then pulled the body towards the bank where Duffield pulled it out to reveal that it was the body of a male infant, naked except for a nappy but with a bag tied around its waist. Francis Shepherd confirmed this testimony and stated that whilst his friend stayed with the child, he had then run off to find a policeman.

Inspector William Moses told the court that he had charge of this case. The body of the child had been brought to him at the police station and he had noted that the bag was tied around the child's waist by means of two pieces of string.

Doctor Timothy Lorkin Walford testified that the last witness, Inspector Moses, had brought the child's body to him and he had therefore performed a post-mortem later that same day. There were no external marks of violence on the child which measured twenty-four inches in length and weighed fifteen pounds. The boy had been well nourished and looked after in life and there were no signs of decomposition. The child's tongue protruded slightly from between his lips but he had not been strangled or asphyxiated. The condition of the lungs showed that the boy had been placed into the water whilst still alive and the cause of death was drowning.

After Samuel Mortlake, the master of the workhouse, had given his testimony, other witnesses from that same establishment were called to confirm his identification of Richard Newell.

Mary Jones was an inmate of the workhouse and had been there since April. She knew Mary Newell very well and had often helped her to nurse her child, after he was born. Besides identifying Richard's body, Mary was also able to say that the bag found around his waist had been made by Mary Newell some two or three weeks before she had left on 9 August.

Harriett Gale was a nurse at the workhouse and had attended Mary Newell during her confinement. She was also able to make a positive identification of the body.

The time came for the child's father to tell his story. Robert William Francis said that he was a poulterer, running his business from a shop in Friar Street. He had first come to know Mary when she was in service and, when she told him she was pregnant, he told her that he was seeing someone else, was about to get engaged and would not help Mary in taking care of the child.

That was the last he saw of her until some time between 7.00pm and 8.00pm on Monday 9 August, when she came into his shop asking him for money. He told her that he had none, and then left the shop. He had not seen her again until now, in court.

After Constable Pitts had given his testimony, the jury retired to consider their verdict. After an absence of only twenty minutes, they returned to say that they had found Mary guilty of murder but wished to add a strong recommendation to mercy. As she received the statutory sentence of death, Mary almost fainted and had to be supported.

In the event, the recommendation of the jury did move the authorities and the death sentence was commuted. Mary was then sent to Reading prison to serve out her sentence. Unfortunately, the birth of her child, the unfeeling attitude of the father, the crime she had committed and the ordeal of arrest, trial and the subsequent death sentence had affected Mary's already fragile mind and she was judged to be insane.

On 4 February 1859, she was transferred to Millbank prison and then, almost immediately, sent to the Fisherton Lunatic Asylum where she remained until December, 1864. By then, she was judged to have recovered somewhat and, on 1 December, was sent back to Millbank. By now she was being considered for eventual release and so, on 1 March 1865, she was transferred to Parkhurst prison for assessment. On 3 July 1866, she was transferred to Brixton where she stayed for two more years, finally being released on 30 November 1868, after serving just over ten years in various institutions. She was now thirty-two years old.

CHAPTER 2

The Reading Baby-farmer Amelia Elizabeth Dyer 1896

On 30 March 1896, a bargeman steering his vessel slowly down the river Thames, between Kennet's Mouth and the Caversham Lock, spotted a brown paper parcel floating in the river. Grabbing his boat-hook, the bargeman snagged the parcel and dragged it towards his boat. Then, as he pulled the sodden bundle from the river, the paper tore and a baby's foot slipped out. The bargeman had just recovered the body of a child.

The tragic parcel was soon handed over to the police and one alert officer, Constable James Anderson, found a label from Temple Meads station in Bristol. He also noticed that there was some faint writing on part of the paper. The cold water of the Thames had all but obliterated the writing but by subjecting it to a microscopic analysis, Anderson was able to decipher a name and an address: Mrs Thomas, Piggott's Road, Lower Caversham. Unfortunately, when that address was checked, officers discovered that Mrs Thomas was no longer there. Meanwhile, using the apparent link to Bristol, officers discovered that a young mother had recently placed a child in the care of a Mrs Thomas. This, in turn, led to the identification of the child found inside the brown paper parcel, as Helena Fry.

The investigation continued and diligent police work soon determined that not only had Mrs Thomas taken in many more children, but also that she had done so under a number of other names. Further, her real name was Amelia Dyer and she had now moved to Kensington Road. A check on her history at Bristol raised a number of concerns. Dyer had a history of mental instability and had been confined to asylums on more than one occasion. It was believed that should she come to think that she was being investigated by the police, Dyer would simply move on yet again. For that reason, a young woman was used as a decoy and arranged a meeting at Dyer's home, ostensibly to discuss placing yet another child in her charge. However, when Mrs Dyer opened the door to her new potential client, at the appointed hour, she was faced instead with two police detectives who said they wanted to interview her about missing children.

The house was searched and much evidence gathered. There were piles of baby clothes in the house and, in addition, officers found letters and telegrams detailing the apparent adoption of dozens of children and babies. However, though the evidence indicated that she should have many children living with her, only two babies were found in the house. Dyer could give no account of what might have happened to all the others and that was enough for the police to arrest her and, on 4 April, she was formally charged with murder.

Since the body of Helena Fry had been found in the river, it was reasonable to assume that if there were any further victims, they too might have been disposed of in the same manner. As a result, officers and others began a systematic dragging of the river.

On 8 April, the decomposed body of a baby boy was recovered. He was never identified. Two days later, another baby boy was found. He too was never identified. That same day, 10 April, a carpet bag was fished out of the Thames. When this was opened, it was found to contain two bodies: a girl, later identified as Doris Marmon and a little boy, identified as Harry Simmons.

Almost two weeks later, on 23 April, a baby identified by a Miss Golding, was recovered from the river. Exactly one week later, on 30 April, yet another unidentified baby boy was found. The body count now stood at seven.

Even before this, the police investigation seemed to indicate that others might have been involved in this awful trade in human life. Dyer's daughter, Mary Ann Palmer and her husband, Arthur, were arrested and may well have faced similar charges to Amelia Dyer, but during the inquests on the various bodies, Dyer wrote a confession, dated 16 April. It read:

Sir, will you kindly grant me the favour of presenting this to the magistrates on Saturday the 18th instant? I have made this statement out, for I may not have the opportunity then. I must relieve my mind. I do know and feel my days are numbered on this earth but I do feel it is an awful thing drawing innocent people into trouble.

I do know I shall have to answer before my Maker in Heaven as on earth, neither my daughter Mary Ann Palmer nor her husband Arthur Ernest Palmer, I do most solemnly declare, neither of them had any thing to do with it. They never knew I contemplated doing such a wicked thing until it was too late. I am speaking the truth and nothing but the truth as I hope to be forgiven. I myself and I alone must stand before my Maker in Heaven, to give an answer for it all.

Witness my hand.
Amelia Dyer.

That letter undoubtedly saved Mary Ann and Arthur Palmer from further investigation on a possible murder charge and the inquest decided that they had not been diectly involved in any of the deaths. However, it was decided to charge Mary Ann Palmer with being an accessory and she was timetabled to face her trial on that charge in June. Dyer, meanwhile, was sent to face her trial on the capital charge.

... fetching a little girl home has me
to go myself but not feeling wel my daughter
has me, I was able to meet her at Reading
... on her return and I can remember her
... me the child, but I dont distinctly know
... was the child I brought up to London
... I take the child home, My daughter
... If I brought her up to London and if I
... that must have been the child I left on the
... the church door, Sometimes I have my
... and I think if that was the first child
... or not any way if It was I can safely
... daughter had nothing whatever to do with
... sure In my own mind she have said
... deal to Screen me and now she is only
... for It herself, suffering for what
... have done, but I am certain now
... tel the truth of the whole matter
... sorry I made such a mistake In my
... tatement and trusting you will beleive me
... no matter what I have done I never did
... aughter or her Husband know the truth
... did do I am telling the truth In this
... never did know,   Amelia Dyer

The confession, written by Amelia Dyer to the authorities, stating that she alone was responsible for killing the children whose bodies had been recovered from the river. The National Archives

In British courts, it is usual to proceed on a single charge of murder, no matter how many actual victims there might have been. Dyer had now been linked directly to seven deaths but it was decided to proceed against her on only one, the murder of Doris Marmon, a child which letters and other evidence could clearly place in Dyer's care. Dyer's trial, on that single charge, opened at the Old Bailey, before Mr Justice Hawkins, on 21 May 1896. During the two days of the proceedings, Dyer was defended by Mr Kapadia and Mr Linford. The case for the Crown rested in the hands of Mr AT Lawrence and Mr Horace Avory. Dyer pleaded guilty to the charge, but claimed that she was insane at the time she committed the crime. That would now be for the jury to decide.

The first witness was Evalina Edith Marmon, the mother of the dead infant. She confirmed that she lived in Cheltenham, had given birth to a baby girl in January and, in March 1896, had seen an advertisement in a newspaper in Bristol. It read: 'Couple with no child, want care of or would adopt one: terms £10. Care of Ship Exchange, Bristol.' Evalina replied to the advertisement and received a letter back, from 45 Kensington Road, Reading. The letter began:

Dear Madam,
In reference to your letter of adoption of a child, I beg to say I shall be happy to have a little baby girl, one that I can bring up and call my own.

First I must tell you, we are plain, homely people, in fairly good circumstances. We live in our own house, and have a good and comfortable home. We are out in the country, and sometimes I am alone a great deal. I don't want the child for money's sake, but for company and home comfort.

Myself and husband are dearly fond of children. None of my own. A child with me would have a good home, and a mother's love and care. We belong to the Church of England.

I would not mind the mother or any friend coming to see the child at any time and know the child is going on all right. I only hope we may come to terms. I should like to have the baby as soon as you can arrange it. If I can come for her, I don't mind paying for one way. I could break my journey at Gloucester; I have a friend in the asylum there I should be so glad to call and see. If you will let me have an early reply I can give you some references.

The letter was signed Mary Harding.

The letter reassured Evalina who replied, saying that she wished to take up the kind offer. On 22 March, she received another letter from Mrs Harding. This began:

Many thanks for your letter of this morning. I shall not answer anyone else till I hear from you again. I assure you I will do my duty to the dear child. I will be a mother as far as possible in my power. If you like to come and stay a few days, or a week, later on, I shall be pleased to make you welcome. It is just lovely here in the summer. There is an orchard opposite our front door. I think Doris a very pretty name; I am sure she ought to be a pretty child.

Other letters were exchanged and final arrangements were made. On Tuesday 31 March, Mrs Harding, who was of course Amelia Dyer, called at Evalina's to pick up the child. An agreement had been drawn up by Evalina which read:

I, Ann Harding, of 45 Kensington Road, Oxford Road, Reading, in consideration of £10 paid to me by E E Marmon, agree to adopt the child and to bring the same up as my own, without any compensation over and above the £10.

Dyer signed that paper and her signature was witnessed by Martha Pockett, Evalina's landlady.

Dyer had promised that she would write to Evalina again just as soon as she arrived back home. A short letter was indeed sent, on 2 April, giving an address in Kensal Rise, in which Dyer claimed that she had been called away to London as her sister had been taken dangerously ill. The child, however, was well and thriving and a much longer letter would follow, once things were back to normal. In fact, no such letter was ever received and Evalina never heard again from Dyer, alias Ann Harding. On 7 April, the police called on Evalina to tell her that they believed her child had been killed. She went up to Reading and formally identified the body on 11 April.

Dyer had not returned to Reading on 31 March after picking up Doris. Mary Ann Beattie testified that at some time after 10.00pm on the night of 31 March, she had been on a bus when she saw Dyer with a large carpet bag and a child. Dyer and Mary Ann alighted from the bus at the same stop on the corner of Mayo Road. Mary Ann noticed Dyer particularly as she appeared to be lost. Mary Ann offered her help and asked Dyer what address she was trying to find. Dyer told her that she was looking for number 76, whereupon Mary Ann not only walked on with her but offered to carry the carpet bag for her.

The next witness was Mary Ann Palmer, Dyer's married daughter. She testified that she lived at 76 Mayo Road, with her husband, and confirmed that Dyer had arrived at her house at around 10.30pm on 31 March. She had a baby girl with her, which was obviously Doris Marmon. Mary had adopted a child herself and, later that night, was putting her baby to bed. At the time, Doris was crying bitterly and Dyer undressed the child in order to quieten it. Some time after this, Mary Ann went up to check on her own child and when she returned, the baby Dyer had with her was lying on the couch, muffled in a shawl and apparently asleep. However, Dyer would not let her daughter go anywhere near the child. The following morning there was no trace of Doris and some tape had disappeared from Mary's workbox.

The suggestion was that Doris Marmon had been murdered

by Dyer that very night. One of the ways that all the murders could be linked back to Dyer was the use of tape tied tightly around their throats. Indeed, at one stage, when she was being interviewed by the police, Dyer had replied that it would be easy to tell which ones she had killed by the tape around their necks.

Doris Marmon's body was eventually discovered, along with that of Harry Simmons, on 10 April. Thus far, the prosecution had indicated that Doris had been killed very soon after Dyer had taken the child from her mother. John Toller, it seems, had come very close to catching Dyer in the very act of disposing of the two bodies.

On the night of Thursday, 2 April, Toller, who worked at the prison at Reading, was walking home after his shift. It was five or perhaps ten minutes to eleven and as he passed the railway arch by the *Rising Sun* public house, he saw a woman approaching him from underneath the arch. That woman was Amelia Dyer and she was walking from the direction of the river.

Henry Smithwaite testified that he had been working with other men, dragging the river on 10 April, when he found a carpet bag near the footbridge at Caversham. The bag was sunk into some twelve feet of water. He managed to hook the bag and drag it to the surface. Knowing full well what it might contain, Smithwaite took the bag to Sergeant Harry James and the two men then opened it together, inside the lock-house.

The bag was tied with string at the top but it still gaped open some three inches or so. The string was cut by Sergeant James and inside the two men saw a piece of brown paper, which covered the rest of the contents. The paper was removed and there lay the body of a female child: Doris Marmon. Sergeant James then reached in and brought out a heavy brick and beneath this lay the body of a male child. The bag was taken to the police station for further investigations.

Doctor William James Morris had examined both bodies in the mortuary at Reading. He noticed that there was a double mark around the neck of the female child, as if a ligature had been tied there quite tightly. The subsequent post-mortem showed that the cause of death had been strangulation. In his opinion, the child had been dead around ten days or so.

Turning to the male child, Dr Morris found a tape ligature still in place. It had been tied twice around the neck, in a bow. Again the cause of death was strangulation and again, the child had been dead for approximately ten days. As for the tape only being found around one of the children's throats, Dyer had since explained that she had simply re-used the one she had killed Doris with.

The time came to raise the subject of the confession Dyer had written for the magistrates. Ellen Gibbs was a matron at Reading prison and had been in charge of Dyer when she penned it. After it was completed, Dyer announced that she had now eased her mind. That same day, Dyer had written a second letter, to her son-in-law, apologising for getting him into trouble and confirming that she had now made a complete confession.

The only hope for Dyer was her plea of insanity and a number of medical men were now called to give their expert opinions on the matter. The first of these witnesses was Dr Frederick Thomas Bishop Logan, who had a practice in Bristol. On Christmas Eve 1893, Dr Logan had been called to examine Dyer at her then home, 114 Wells Road, but she had rushed at him with a poker and threatened to break his skull. She told him that she had heard voices telling her to kill herself. Dr Logan believed that she was of unsound mind and had written out a certificate to that effect, which committed her to an asylum.

Dr J Lacy Firth was in charge of Dyer at the Bristol General Hospital. On 26 April 1894, Dyer had been brought to the hospital after she had apparently tried to drown herself. She stayed in his care for thirteen days during which time she was questioned about a missing child. Dr Firth was unable to recall any other details of the case.

Doctor William Frederick Bailey Eden was a surgeon, and on 14 December 1894, he had been called to examine Dyer in

Fishponds. She offered him violence, but he allowed her to talk on and came to the conclusion that she was of unsound mind. Once again, Dyer was sent to an asylum, but was discharged in January 1895.

Doctor Forbes Winslow had examined Dyer in Holloway prison on 15 May 1896, just a few days before the trial began. He had specifically asked her about the two children whose bodies had been found together in the river. Dyer's answers were vague and she seemed to have little or no recollection of names, dates, times and places. In Dr Winslow's opinion too, Dyer was of unsound mind.

So far, all the medical evidence had appeared to confirm the plea of insanity, but other testimony now negated this. Doctor James Scott was the medical officer at Holloway and he had been observing Dyer since her admission there on 7 May. In his opinion, she was perfectly sane.

Doctor Henry Savage testified that he had seventeen years of medical experience in treating various forms of lunacy. He had examined Dyer, for one hour only, at Holloway, and concluded that she was not mentally unsound.

The final witness of all was not a medical expert. James Hobley was Dyer's brother and he made it clear that he wanted nothing to do with the case. In reply to the first question put to him he replied: 'I wish my name not to be mentioned in public. I shall be a pensioner. I am the prisoner's brother. My mother was never insane. There was never a case of insanity in our family.' Finally, in response to a question from Mr Kapadia for the defence, Hobley said: 'I have not seen the prisoner for thirty-five or thirty-six years. She is a total stranger to me.'

Having heard all the evidence, the jury took just six minutes to decide that Amelia Dyer was guilty as charged, perfectly sane and so responsible for her actions. She was then sentenced to death and moved to the condemned cell at Newgate to await her appointment with the hangman.

An interesting point of law was then raised. It was still the

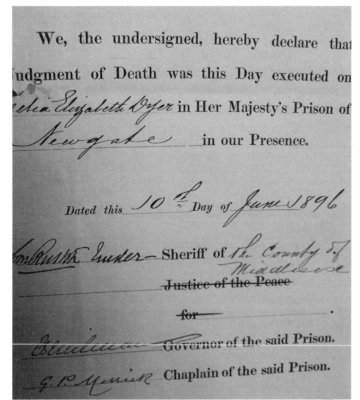

The notice of execution from Newgate prison. The National Archives

intention of the authorities to prosecute Dyer's daughter, Mary Ann Palmer, for being an accessory. Her trial was due to open on 16 June and, of course, the chief witness against her would have been her own mother, Amelia Dyer.

Attempts were made to serve a subpoena on Dyer, inside her cell, but the prison authorities refused to accept it and notified the Home Office of the event. Documents preserved in The National Archives at Kew show that it was decided that no subpoena could circumnavigate or delay a sentence of death and the prison was right in refusing to accept it. Since, by the time Mary Ann's case would come to court, the chief witness against her would be dead, no further action was taken against Dyer's daughter.

Newgate prison where Amelia Dyer was executed. Author's Collection

What followed was a very busy time for the authorities at Newgate with four executions within two days. On 9 June, three men, Henry Fowler, Albert Milsom and William Seaman, had all been hanged there. The following day, 10 June, they were followed to the gallows by fifty-seven-year-old Amelia Elizabeth Dyer. She was hanged for the murder of Doris Marmon, with six more deaths directly attributed to her; but in reality, the police had come to believe that many more infant deaths, over a long period of time, might have been due to the crimes of the Reading baby-farmer.

CHAPTER 3

Executions at Reading

Since the year 1800, there have been a total of thirty-five executions at Reading. Twenty-seven of these took place in public, with the remaining eight taking place in private within the precincts of the prison.

Public Executions

Given below are the basic details of the twenty-seven public executions:

John Holt – Hanged 6 March 1800, for murder
James Durner – Hanged 19 July 1801, for murder
Edward Painter – Hanged 29 March 1802, for cattle theft
John Ryan – Hanged 30 July 1802, for murder
Dennis Daley – Hanged 19 March 1803, for forgery
Thomas Cox – Hanged 23 March 1811, for bestiality
Charles White – Hanged 26 March 1814, for horse theft
John Newbank – Hanged 25 March 1815, for uttering a forged
    document
James Castle – Hanged 2 August 1817, for sheep theft
Thomas Ayres – Hanged 10 August 1818, for burglary
Edward Tooley – Hanged 7 August 1819, for burglary
David Patience – Also hanged 7 August 1819, for burglary
George Wiggins – Hanged 18 March 1820, for highway
    robbery
Daniel Grimshaw – Hanged 4 March 1824, for murder

William Giles – Hanged 28 May 1827, for uttering a forged
   document

Samuel Wright – Hanged 22 March 1828, for shooting a gun
   at a person

Henry Burnett – Hanged alongside Wright, above, for the same
   offence

Thomas Field – Also hanged alongside Wright, for the same
   offence

William Winterburn – Hanged 11 January 1831, for riot

Edward Green – Hanged 4 August 1832, for burglary

Thomas Lincoln – Hanged alongside Green, above, for the
   same offence

James Morris – Also hanged alongside Green, for the same
   offence

John Carter – Hanged 16 March 1833, for arson

George King – Hanged 3 March 1834, for murder

Thomas Jennings – Hanged 22 March 1845, for murder

William Spicer – Hanged 20 March 1846, for murder

John Gould – Hanged 14 March 1862, for murder

Private Executions

All eight executions within Reading prison were for murder and
none were for crimes actually committed within the town itself.
The details are:

Francis and Henry Tidbury – 12 March 1877

In the early hours of 11 December 1876, Constable Thomas
Golby was patrolling a lonely lane in Hungerford when he found
the dead body of a brother officer, Constable Shorter, at the
entrance to some woods.

Having attracted the attention of a local gamekeeper, Golby
then went to the police station to report what he had found.
There he was informed that Inspector Drewatt had also been in
that area and had not reported back to the station. A search was

then organised to find the missing officer. Eventually, his body was also found, not far from Constable Shorter's. Both men had been shot.

When officers spoke to the gamekeeper, he reported that he had seen two local men, William Day and William Tidbury, leaving the woods soon after Constable Golby had gone for help. These two men were well known in the locale as poachers and very soon they were placed under arrest, along with two other known members of their gang: Francis Tidbury and Henry Tidbury, both brothers of William.

The clothing of all four men bore traces of blood and when their boots were checked, they were seen to match impressions left at the scene of the two shootings. The final piece of evidence was a cap, belonging to Henry Tidbury, found beneath the body of Inspector Drewatt.

The trial of the four men took place on 19 February 1877, before Mister Justice Lindsay. In the meantime, Henry Tidbury had made a full confession claiming that he and his brother Francis had shot the two officers whilst the two other poachers were outside the woods. He explained that they had taken two pheasants and were on their way home, when they were stopped by Inspector Drewatt. They knew that he had recognised them so shot him dead in order to make good their escape. Just minutes later, Constable Shorter came upon the scene so they had little alternative but to shoot him too.

None of the four defendants managed to escape punishment. William Day and William Tidbury were both sent to prison whilst the other two were sentenced to death. Francis Tidbury was hanged on his twenty-seventh birthday, alongside his twenty-four-year-old brother.

John Carter – 5 December 1893

Carter lived with his third wife at Bronledge Farm, Watchfield, near Farringdon. On the night of 20 June 1893, Carter's son heard loud banging and the sound of an argument, coming from his parents' bedroom. The next morning, Carter told his son that he was not allowed to enter the bedroom and it was obvious that something had been burnt in the fireplace.

It was then that Carter began to tell people that his wife had gone to stay with some relatives. This, added to what the son had heard the previous night, raised suspicions and the police were informed that something might well have happened to Mrs Carter. A search of the farm was made, and there officers found the body of Mrs Carter buried beneath the washroom floor. She had been beaten to death and her body then burned.

Faced with this evidence, Carter then surprised the officers by admitting to not one murder, but two. He made a full confession stating that the body of his missing second wife was also buried within the house. In due course, her skeleton was recovered and, after the formality of a trial, Carter was hanged in December.

Charles Thomas Wooldridge – 7 July 1896

Wooldridge's crime was nothing out of the ordinary; another story of unrequited love and jealousy ending in murder. It lives on, not because of his actions, but because of a long poem, written by another inmate of the prison, where he finally paid the penalty for what he had done.

Wooldridge was a soldier, serving in the Royal Horse Guards at Windsor and it was there that he met his future wife, Laura Glendell, who worked at the post office in the High Street, Eton. As a soldier, Wooldridge required his commanding officer's permission to marry, but failed to obtain this. As a result, he and Laura married in secret and Laura continued to use her maiden name.

The couple lived at 21 Alma Terrace, Arthur Road, Windsor but the love match soon proved to be something else, for Wooldridge had a violent temper, especially when he was in drink. Then came another problem in the form of a posting for Wooldridge, to Regent's Park in London. Since he had not received permission to marry, the army did not recognise his union with Laura, and so she was unable to accompany him to the capital. The parting was not on the best of terms and soon afterwards, Laura began seeing another soldier, a corporal in the Life Guards.

Wooldridge knew nothing of this new emotional attachment, and believed that it was only a matter of time before he and Laura would be back together again. On Sunday 29 March 1896, he made an arrangement to meet her outside his barracks in London, but Laura failed to attend. Soon after this he heard, from a friend, that Laura was seeing someone else. As far as Wooldridge was concerned, that was the final straw.

That same day, 29 March, Wooldridge borrowed a cut-throat razor from another soldier and made the trip back to Windsor. There he called at 21 Alma Terrace, saying that he needed her to sign some papers. Laura let her husband into the house and immediately he drew out the razor and slashed her throat.

The stricken woman managed to rush out into the street but Wooldridge followed her, caught up with her and slashed her throat twice more. As a crowd gathered around the scene, Wooldridge calmly gave himself up to the first police officer on the scene, Constable Henry Miles, with the words: 'Take me, I have killed my wife.'

Convicted of murder, Wooldridge was sent to Reading to await his execution. There, one day whilst he was on exercise, he was seen by a fellow prisoner, Oscar Wilde, who would later pen the famous poem, *The Ballad of Reading Gaol*, which he would dedicate to Wooldridge. Wilde wrote in his poem:

> *And each man kills the thing he loves*
> *By each let this be heard,*
> *Some do it with a bitter look,*
> *Some with a flattering word,*
> *The coward does it with a kiss,*
> *The brave man with a sword*

Charles Scott – 28 November 1899

In some ways, Scott's crime was similar to Wooldridge's but no poem exists to immortalise it.

Scott and his wife also lived in Windsor and both were addicted to drink. On 2 September 1899, they went out drinking together and an argument ensued. At one stage, Scott drew out a razor and slashed his wife's throat. Like Wooldridge he then waited calmly until a police constable appeared, and gave himself up. He was hanged, in November, by James Billington.

William George Thomas Charles Austin – 5 November 1907

On Tuesday 16 July 1907, thirteen-year-old Unity Annie Butler returned to school at 1.30pm after having her lunch at home, 5 Cranbourne Terrace, Clewer, Windsor.

Later that same day, at around 5.30pm, Unity's father, William, arrived home from work to find his lodger, William Austin, busily polishing his boots. There was no sign of Unity in the house, but her father assumed she had simply gone on an errand with her mother. At around 6.00pm, Austin left the house, but returned after a few minutes to collect his bicycle. He then rode away, never to return to Cranbourne Terrace.

It was almost 11.00pm when Mrs Butler finally arrived home and clearly, Unity was not with her. A search was organised and it did not take long to find the missing child. Her partially clothed and strangled body was found underneath William Austin's bed.

The police investigation soon found a witness. Ludwig Poegell, a neighbour, said that he had heard screams coming from the Butlers' house, at 4.30pm. It was now imperative to find the missing lodger, William Austin, who also used the name William Saunders.

In fact, Austin had been seen, earlier that night, at 9.30pm, by a friend of his, Walter West. Austin seemed to be rather upset and when West asked him what the problem was, Austin replied that he had committed a crime and the only way out now was for him to drown himself. He would not tell West what the crime actually was but once West heard about Unity's murder, he contacted the police and told them what he had seen.

Austin was traced and arrested. Taken to the police station, he was searched as a matter of routine and officers found a letter, addressed to Unity's parents, apologising for what he had done to their daughter. It was as good as a written confession.

Austin's trial took place on 14 October, before Mister Justice Jelf and here the defence tried to claim that Unity had been rather 'fast'. Apparently she had often spent time in Austin's room when they were alone in the house and had sat on his bed, seeming to entice him.

On the day of the attack, Unity had sneered at Austin and called him names. He lost his temper, grabbed her and, before he knew what was happening, he had taken a piece of rope and strangled her. This did not explain, however, how some of Unity's clothing had been removed.

The jury had little difficulty in returning a guilty verdict, and Austin was hanged, on Bonfire night, by Henry and Thomas Pierrepoint.

William Broome – 24 November 1910

Seventy-year-old Isabella Wilson ran a second-hand clothes shop from 22 High Street, Slough and was well known to her neighbours and fellow shopkeepers.

On Friday 15 July 1910, one of those neighbours, Mrs White, had something she wished to talk to Isabella about. It was 7.00pm when Mrs White walked towards the shop but there was a bicycle parked against the window. It was clear that Isabella had a customer and Mrs White did not wish to discuss her business in front of a stranger so she decided to leave things until later.

At 8.00pm, Mrs White returned. The bicycle had gone and, going into the shop, Mrs White called out for her friend. There was no reply, for there, on the floor in the sitting-room, at the back of the shop, lay the body of Isabella Wilson.

At first the police believed that Isabella had been strangled but a subsequent post-mortem revealed that she had actually been smothered. Isabella had been struck a number of times, bound and gagged, and a cushion forced into her mouth. That cushion had prevented her from breathing and led directly to her death.

The motive for the crime was easy to detect. Isabella had been in the habit of wrapping her gold coins in paper and then stuffing them into her purse. That purse was now empty but close by lay a piece of paper that bore the impression of nineteen coins: seventeen large and two small. Those impressions were the size of sovereigns and half sovereigns.

Other shopkeepers in the area were questioned and they told of a man seen loitering around Isabella's shop at around 1.00pm. Further, some of the shopkeepers were able to recall that at one stage this man had been a lodger at the premises next door to the shop. It was easy, therefore, to put a name to him: William Broome who also used the name Brooks.

Further investigations revealed that Broome was now living in London but when he was interviewed he denied being in Slough on the day Isabella had met her death. Unfortunately, the officers noticed that there were two parallel scratches on Broome's face, which might well have been caused by fingernails. Asked to explain them, Broome said he had been in a fight in Camden Town on Saturday 10 July. Nevertheless, Broome was cautioned and a search of his rooms carried out. There police found nineteen sovereigns and two half-sovereigns. Broome was arrested and charged with murder.

At first, Broome stuck to his claim that he had not been in Slough on the day of the murder. He said he had been out looking for work from around 10.20am until 1.00pm. Then he had gone to the *Trafalgar* public house in St Martin's Lane where he had some bread and cheese for lunch. From there he went to 146 Albany Street, where he read a newspaper before going back to his lodgings.

The police investigation was certainly a thorough one and this led to two chemists being traced. The first, who had an establishment at Paddington station, said that Broome had called at some time before 3.00pm asking for a lotion that might remove scratches from his face. The second, who traded from Oxford Street, said that Broome came in at 5.00pm where he bought a lotion and some cotton wool.

The witnesses, who said they had seen Broome in Slough, were spoken to again and confirmed that he had no scratches on his face at 1.00pm. Finally, Anna Lextus, Broome's landlady, said she had seen Broome after 5.00pm on 15 July and had remarked on the scratches on his face. Broome had joked that he hoped people didn't think he had been robbing an old lady of her money.

All this evidence was put before Broome, who now made a second statement. In this he claimed that he had caught a train from Paddington to Windsor intending to visit the headquarters of the Yeomanry, for which he was a reservist. That building was closed so he went on to Slough, where he arrived some time between noon and 1.00pm. He had not, however, robbed or killed Isabella Wilson.

Broome's trial took place at Aylesbury on 14 October before Mister Justice Bucknill and lasted for two days. At that trial, the defence missed picking up on one vitally important piece of evidence.

Throughout the proceedings the prosecution referred again and again to the piece of paper found at the crime scene and claimed that the gold coins found in Broome's lodgings matched this number exactly. However, the paper had borne nineteen impressions; presumably of seventeen sovereigns and two halves but nineteen sovereigns and two halves had been found in London. It was true that Broome may well have stolen the coins from Isabella and had two sovereigns of his own but this was not the point. The prosecution claimed that the match was exact.

Despite this, and other possible doubts about the case, Broome was found guilty of murder and executed on Thursday 24 November by John Ellis and William Willis.

Eric James Sedgewick – 4 February 1913

Twenty-two-year-old Annie Wentworth Davis was working in Cotton Hall House, Eton Wick Road, Eton, for the second time in her young life. Her first period of employment there had ended in December 1907 but in August 1912 she had returned. There she became very friendly with another servant, Edith Alice Armstrong. The two young ladies chatted about all the different aspects of their lives and one of the things Annie told Edith about was the man in her life: twenty-nine-year-old Eric Sedgewick.

Annie said she had first met Eric in January 1908. He had been a soldier but had been discharged, on 4 February 1902, with an excellent record. Annie, however, had her concerns and she told Edith that she had seen another side to Eric; a rather volatile temper.

The household at Cotton Hall House soon saw some evidence of this temper for themselves. In October 1912, Eric sent Annie a telegram saying that he was coming to Eton from London, where he lived, and would meet her. Unfortunately he had not waited for a reply because Annie was busy with her duties and couldn't simply leave without permission. As a consequence, she was not at the arranged rendezvous and Eric duly appeared at Cotton Hall House, clearly in the most furious of tempers.

On 10 November, Eric travelled up to Eton again and this time the couple did meet. Immediately afterwards, Edith Armstrong and others noticed a change in Annie. Though she did not tell her friends what the problem was, correspondence between Annie and Eric, found later by the police, would tell the whole story.

On that visit, Annie had apparently surrendered herself to Eric for the first time. However, that very same night, Eric had also confessed to Annie that he had been unfaithful to her. She brooded on the matter that night and the following morning wrote to Eric to tell him that it was over between them. She also told her friend, Edith, that Eric had told her something which would worry her to her grave.

Eric tried his best to rekindle the relationship. He wrote to Annie on 19 November saying that he loved her dearly. She thought about this for some days before replying, on 23 November, saying that she hadn't changed her mind and confirming that it was all over.

The following day, Sunday 24 November 1912, Eric travelled from London to Eton. He arrived at Cotton Hall House at 3.50pm and it was Edith who answered the door when he rang the bell. At his request, she went to tell Annie that Eric was there. Annie, knowing that Eric had a temper, seemed frightened and asked Edith if she would go back downstairs with her. Edith did as her friend asked but, when they had all been together for a few minutes and Eric still seemed calm, Edith left them alone in the servant's hall.

Edith returned to her own duties in the kitchen. Then, after some minutes, she went back into the servant's hall where she found, to her horror, Annie slumped in a chair with blood pouring from a wound in her left breast. Eric was standing over her shouting hysterically: 'She's not dead! She's not dead!' As other servants rushed to take Eric from the room he was heard to cry: 'For God's sake, can't somebody stop the bleeding?'

Annie did not recover from her wound and Eric was duly arrested and charged with her murder. He appeared before Mister Justice Bankes, at Aylesbury, on 15 January 1913 and was found guilty of wilful murder. He was hanged on Tuesday 4 February, by John Ellis and George Brown, and became the last man to ever be executed at Reading. It was eleven years to the day since Eric Sedgewick had received his honourable discharge from the army.

CHAPTER 4

A New Life
Ada Jane Cook
1918

On 12 June 12 1915, Ada Cook, an unmarried domestic servant, gave birth to a healthy baby boy, who she named Stanley. For a couple of years, Ada managed to take care of the child herself. They lived with Ada's mother but, in the autumn of 1917, Ada's mother died and so, on 24 August 1917, when Stanley was two years old, he was taken to the house of Ann Caroline Brooker, Ada's aunt, at 19 Foundry Street, Reading.

The terms of the arrangement were that Ada would pay Ann Brooker four shillings per week for the child's upkeep. This was not really a problem for Ada, because, in September 1917, she obtained employment at a factory close to Ann's home. As a result, Ada also moved in with her aunt and increased the weekly payments to fourteen shillings to cover both her and her son.

Ada had made a mistake by getting herself pregnant but now, slowly, she was getting on her feet. In January 1918, she moved out of her aunt's house, leaving her son behind, and took lodgings with William and Maria Priest at 30 Castle Street, also in Reading. It seemed, at last, that life was improving for Ada Cook but then, in March, things all began to go wrong.

It was on 10 March 1918, that Ann Brooker appeared at Ada's new lodgings in Castle Street. She had Stanley with her and explained that he was now getting too big for her to look after. She was sorry, but Ada would have to take the child back and have him live with her. Faced with this dilemma, Ada begged Maria Priest to allow him to stay there, until she could get something more permanent sorted out. Reluctantly, Maria Priest agreed but made it plain that she was far from happy with the arrangement; a lodger was one thing but a lodger with a young child was quite another.

In fact this new arrangement lasted all of two days. On 12 March, Maria Priest explained that she had spoken to her husband at length and decided that the boy had to go and, if Ada couldn't make new arrangements immediately, then she would have to go too.

At her wit's end, Ada took Stanley back to her aunt's house and begged her to take him back. She explained that she would be turned out of her lodgings if Ann Brooker refused the request, but Ann was adamant. She had made her decision and could not have Stanley back.

It seemed, though, that Ada Cook did find a solution after all. When she returned to Maria Priest's house that same evening, there was no child with her and Ada explained that she had found him a very comfortable place where he would be well looked after.

Once again Ada's life appeared to be improving for, on 3 April 1918, she found new employment as a domestic at the Women's Training Colony at Cope Hall, Newbury. Further she could live in there and, it seems, was well liked by all the students and staff. At long last, her troubles all seemed to be behind her.

Frederick Charles Watson was the resident foreman at Huntley and Palmer's factory and lived on the premises at 2 Gasworks Road, Reading. On 7 April, he was fishing in the river Kennet when he spotted what appeared to be the body of a large dog, floating in the water. Disgusted that some vandal could just dump an animal in this way, Frederick took his boat, rowed out to the bundle and then dragged it to the shore. Once there it became clear that the bundle was not a dead dog but the body of a male child. He immediately ran for the police.

The first officer on the scene was Constable William Kerry, who timed his arrival at 10.00am. He did not disturb the bundle but carried it to the mortuary in Bridge Street. It was there that the body was examined, by Dr Percy William House.

The child was fully dressed with a coat placed over the face and the sleeves wrapped around and tied about the neck. A scarf had also been tied tightly over the boy's mouth and nose, and when this was removed, Dr House found that a handkerchief had been stuffed tightly into his mouth. The post-mortem showed that death had been due to suffocation.

The boy was identified as Stanley Cook within a very short time, due to the fact that his mother had actually been taken into custody earlier and questioned about his disappearance.

On 25 March, Ada Cook had visited 305 Oxford Road, the home of William Bansor the local inspector for the Society for the Prevention of Cruelty to Children. She explained that she had just been to her aunt's house in Foundry Street and tried to collect some child's clothing. Her aunt had not believed her story that Stanley was now being looked after in a good home and demanded more details before she would hand over any of the child's belongings. Ada had now called on Mr Bansor to ask him for a note so that she could go back and get the items belonging to her son.

Far from being satisfied with this explanation, Mr Bansor himself demanded to know where the child was. Ada explained that she had taken Stanley to a woman in Newbury who had contacts in certain children's homes in London. Stanley was now in one of those homes but when asked for more details, Ada was somewhat vague. As a result, Mr Banson escorted Ada to the police station for interview.

At the station, Ada was seen by Detective Constable Charles Henderson. Here she told the same story, but claimed not to know the name of the woman in Newbury, or the address of the home in London. As a result, Ada appeared in court two days later, on 27 March, on a charge of child abandonment. She was remanded to 3 April but on that date, as no evidence was offered, was discharged.

To be absolutely sure that the child found in the Kennet was actually Stanley, Ann Brooker was taken to the Bridge Street mortuary to view the body. She positively identified the child as Stanley and so, on that same day, 7 April, Ada Cook was arrested at the Women's Training Colony by Constable Henderson.

Ada faced her trial for murder, at Reading, on 4 June 1918. The presiding judge was Mr Justice Lawrence and the case for the Crown was outlined by Mr HJ Farrant. Ada's defence rested in the hands of Mr McKenna.

In addition to the witnesses already referred to, the prosecution called Frederick Durston Whitcombe, a senior warder at Reading prison. He told the court that he was in Forbury Road at around 6.25pm on 12 March and, as he passed over Plates Bridge, he saw a woman with a child. He noticed them in particular because they were walking down the tow path towards the river and he thought it strange that an unaccompanied woman should be in such a place at that time.

Whitcombe watched as the woman turned towards Addis Square and in all, he observed her for some fifty yards. On 8 April, he attended an identity parade of nine women and without hesitation picked out Ada Cook as the woman he had seen. The defence tried their best to discredit Whitcombe's testimony, stating that it was dark in that area and there were large trees overhanging the tow path but they failed to shake him in any way.

It was no surprise when the jury announced their verdict; Ada was guilty of the murder of her son. She was then sentenced to death and moved to Oxford prison to await execution.

An appeal was entered and this was heard on 24 June 1918, by Mr Justice Bray, Mr Justice Darling and Mr Justice Coleridge. Much was made of the state of mind of the prisoner at the time she committed this awful crime, but the judges were not to be moved and the death sentence was confirmed.

Ada Cook did not hang, however. Her sentence was commuted to one of life imprisonment and she was taken from the condemned cell at Oxford and moved to Liverpool to serve out her sentence.

Every single year, Ada petitioned the Home Office for her release. She admitted that she had done a terrible thing, but had been driven to it out of sheer desperation. She was truly sorry for what she had done and wished to rebuild her life as soon as she possibly could.

Mr Justice Darling, one of the Appeal Court judges who confirmed Ada Cook's death sentence. Author's Collection

By 1921, the authorities had decided that there should be a minimum tariff in this case of ten years' imprisonment. However, Ada was told that she could be released on licence after six and two-thirds years, providing she behaved herself whilst in custody.

Ada did indeed prove to be a model prisoner and by 1923, she was being prepared for release. There was however one problem, not made public at the time but certainly mentioned in the various Home Office and prison authority communications. It was believed that the father of Ada's child was none other than her own father, a drunken brute of a man with many convictions for assault. He was now living in Henley and the authorities were determined that Ada should not return to his care.

Eventually, a place was found for Ada and on 13 May 1923, she was released on licence. She took a position as a domestic servant in one of the Thompson's Homes at 4 Liverpool Street, King's Cross, London. Finally she could start to rebuild her life.

CHAPTER 5

Avoiding the Noose
Edith Agnes Loader
1919

On 29 March 1918, twenty-six-year-old Edith Loader gave birth to a child, a girl, at her married sister's house in Oxted. The child was named Maisie Clough Loader, the middle name of the baby being a clue to the identity of her father.

In 1917, Edith had been living with her mother in Manchester. Another lodger at the house had been a Staff Sergeant named Clough, and Edith and he had started walking out together. In due course, Edith had discovered that she was pregnant, but by now, Clough had left Manchester and all attempts to trace him had failed. It was to avoid a scandal that Edith had then travelled to the home of Florence Louisa Turner, her sister, for the latter part of the confinement.

After the birth, mother and child both stayed with Florence Turner until 25 April. On that date, Edith left Florence's home but couldn't return to her mother's house because, in the meantime, that lady had died. Instead, Edith went to live with another married sister, Mrs Reid. Little Maisie was left with Florence Turner and her husband. That arrangement did not last long, however, for in July 1918, Edith collected her four-month-old daughter and moved down to Reading in order to make a fresh start.

Edith and Maisie had no home to actually go to in Reading and that was why they eventually fell upon the mercy of the Salvation Army. Maria Goodyer was the caretaker for the Army at 123 Queen's Road, Reading, and she first met Edith on 9 October, when she called and asked to speak to one of the officers. Unfortunately, all of the officers were away at the time and there was therefore no-one to help Edith or offer her any advice.

Maria next saw Edith on 13 October when they met, by arrangement in, of all places, the local cemetery. After listening to Edith's story, Maria took the mother and child back to Queen's Road. They were allowed board and lodgings and, in return, Edith did whatever work Maria asked of her. For a time at least, things seemed to be progressing well and by all accounts, Edith appeared to be a most devoted mother.

The problem was that with a young baby to take care of, Edith could not find real work for herself and so, in turn, was unable to establish a proper new life. The solution, obviously, was to find a home for Maisie in order that Edith could make a proper career for herself.

A temporary solution presented itself in mid-October when Edith was able to leave the child with Miss Margaret Esther Payne, the Superintendent of the East Reading Day Nursery, but this only lasted for three days, from 18 October until 21 October. After that time, Edith asked if she could leave Maisie there permanently but was told that this was not possible.

Maria Goodyer knew very well that Edith was trying to find a permanent home for the baby and was somewhat relieved when, on 21 October, Edith left the Salvation Army Home with Maisie but returned that evening without her. Edith informed Maria that she had, at last, found a foster mother to take permanent care of the little girl. Asked for further details, Edith told Maria that Maisie was with a Mrs Page who lived in Chumleigh Road.

Free of the burden of the baby, Edith now began to improve her life. Two days after Maisie had been placed with Mrs Page, Edith obtained employment as a domestic servant with a nurse,

Anne Marie Barker, and moved in to her house on 23 October. At last, Edith was getting on her feet.

It was on 9 November that James Midwinter, a gardener living in Henley-on-Thames, found the body of a little girl floating in the river near Shiplake Lock at Wargrave. The child was wearing a blue spotted frock, a blue striped petticoat, a white petticoat underneath, a lace pinafore, a flannel chemise and woollen leggings, knickers and bonnet.

Midwinter ran for the police and the first officer on the scene was Constable Ernest Thatcher, who collected the body and took it to the mortuary. A post-mortem was carried out by Dr FC Young, who confirmed that the cause of death was drowning. The problem now was identifying the poor child.

As a matter of routine, all women who were known to have young children were spoken to. This was the reason that caused Sergeant James Pierce to call at Miss Barker's house on 16 November. Edith was spoken to and asked what had happened to her child. She again told the story of Maisie being placed with Mrs Page, but when Sergeant Pierce went to check he found that not only was there no trace of Maisie, but there was no trace of a Mrs Page either. That same day, Edith was taken into custody but she was not held in jail or even in the police cells. Instead, Edith was given over to the care of Elizabeth Haddrell, the wife of Inspector Haddrell who was based at Wokingham.

The investigation continued and any establishments that might possibly deal with young children were spoken too and that included the Salvation Army at Reading. Maria Goodyer thought that the description of the clothing might well match items which she had seen Maisie Loader dressed in. Three days after the child's body had been found, the tragic bundle had been buried in Wargrave churchyard but the baby was now exhumed and, on 27 November, Maria viewed the body and made a positive identification. The child found at Wargrave was indeed Maisie Loader and Edith was then charged with murder.

Edith Loader appeared to face the charge, at Reading before

Mr Justice Rowlatt, on 15 January 1919. The case for the prosecution rested in the hands of Mr Jordan whilst Edith was defended by Mr Snagge.

There really was little hope for the defence since Edith had confessed her guilt to two people. The first of these was Mrs Haddrell, the wife of the police inspector. Whilst Edith was in her care she had said:

> *I was driven by desperation to do it. I went down to the river two or three times to do it and the third time I laid my baby in the river.*
>
> *I kissed her. Then I realised what I had done and I tried to reach her but could not, the stream having washed her too far away. I loved my baby very much indeed. I am very sorry for what I have done.*

Edith had also confessed to Sergeant Pierce, whilst being interviewed by him. She said to him: 'I have done it in desperation. I was desperate at the time. I put it in the water two days before I came here, down by the ice factory. I have been sorry ever since I done it.'

The jury had little trouble in adjudging Edith to be guilty of murder but they did add a strong recommendation to mercy. After all, everyone had said that she was a most loving mother and she had apparently been driven to this out of desperation. The law, however, only allowed for one possible sentence and the judge donned the black cap and sentenced Edith to death by hanging. She was then sent to Oxford prison to await her fate.

The very next day, 16 January, Mr Justice Rowlatt presided over another murder trial at the same Reading assizes. Joseph Rose was accused of killing his girlfriend, Sarah Rose, who also happened to be his cousin, and their five-month-old daughter, Isabella, by cutting their throats near Newbury. He too was found guilty and sentenced to death and he too was sent to Oxford to await his fate.

On Wednesday 19 February, Joseph Rose was hanged at Oxford by John Ellis and Edward Taylor. Edith Loader, however, managed to avoid the hangman's noose as her sentence was commuted to life imprisonment, just five days after her trial, on 20 January 1919 and she was transferred to Liverpool to serve out her sentence.

Although Edith should have served a long prison term, the authorities did look upon her with mercy. She only served a little more than four years, being released on licence on 18 April 1923. She would never forget the child she had loved so much.

CHAPTER 6

A Gentleman of the Theatre
The Murder of Alfred Oliver
1929

Alfred Oliver had not had the happiest of lives. His first wife had drowned herself after the death of their only child, but things had begun to improve for him when he met and married his second wife, Annie Elizabeth, in 1920. The couple lived a quiet enough life and friends would say that they were deliriously happy together. Now, in 1929, Alfred ran his tobacconist's shop from 15 Cross Street, Reading, whilst his wife ran a corsetiere business from the house at the back.

At around 5.00pm on Saturday 22 June 1929, Alfred went into the dining room behind the shop, with Annie, for his evening meal. After they had finished, Annie Elizabeth took over in the shop whilst Alfred cleared the crockery away and, during the next twenty-five minutes or so, served six male customers.

Once he had finished, Alfred returned to his duties behind the shop counter whilst his wife went upstairs. It was then some five or ten minutes before 6.00pm, and soon afterwards, Annie heard the clock strike six.

It was about then that Annie took the dog through the yard at the back of the shop, and took it for a short walk. She was gone for perhaps fifteen minutes, during which she heard no sounds of any disturbance. It was around 6.15pm when she went back inside.

The shop in Cross Street, Reading, where Alfred Oliver was attacked. Author's Collection

Annie called out for her husband, but there was no reply. She noticed that the door, which separated the shop from the dining room, was closed. That was strange, for Alfred always kept the door open in the summer. Annie pushed the door open and saw Alfred, sitting with his back to the shop fittings. Alfred held a handkerchief to his mouth and a pool of blood lay on the floor nearby, with a pair of broken false teeth resting in the crimson liquid. To the left, Annie saw a pair of broken glasses and part of a set of scales, which were normally kept on the counter. Alfred was obviously hurt but when Annie asked him what had happened, he could only reply: 'I don't know, darling.'

Alfred Oliver, the dead man.
Author's Collection

Anne didn't touch anything and ran to George Taylor's cafe at 29 Cross Street. Both Mr Taylor and his wife, Nellie, went back to the tobacconist's to see if they could offer any assistance. Anne and George lifted Alfred by gently grabbing him beneath the arms and placing him in a chair in the dining room at the back of the shop. Meanwhile, the doctor was sent for.

Constable Frank Chandler was off duty and shopping at 19 Cross Street when Nellie Taylor rushed in. She was very agitated and asked the manager to telephone for the police. No sooner had she said this, than she recognised Chandler and asked him to come back to the shop with her, saying that Mr Oliver had been attacked and was badly hurt.

Constable Chandler followed Nellie back to the tobacconist's and saw Alfred, in a chair in the back room. The poor man was still bleeding rather badly from a head wound but Chandler, having made a quick search of the shop, found no weapon, which might have accounted for the injuries Alfred had suffered.

The inside of the shop where the attack took place. Author's Collection

Another view of the inside of Alfred Oliver's shop, showing the stock shelves. Author's Collection

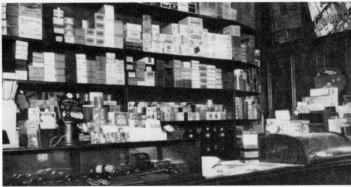

Told that the police and a doctor had been sent for, Chandler then waited until more senior officers arrived.

The next officer on the scene was Detective Sergeant Oliver Pope. He noted blood splashes on the showcases and the stock at the rear of the shop. He also saw a broken pair of scales on the floor and smears of blood on the outside of a carton of cigarettes. There was no sign of any struggle, and the stock was apparently undisturbed.

In due course, the Chief Constable, Thomas Alfred Burrows, arrived at the shop. He spoke to Alfred, who was still semi-conscious, and asked him what had happened. Alfred managed to reply: 'There was a man came in. I thought he was from the gas office.'

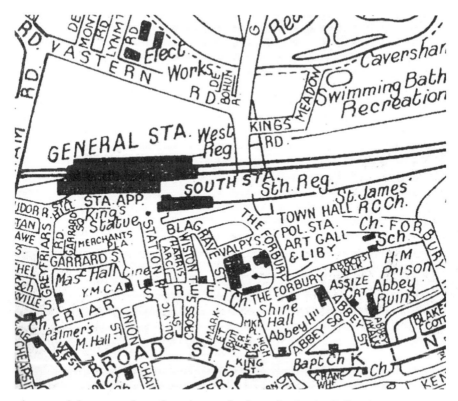

A map of the area where the crime took place. Author's Collection

Alfred said that he didn't wish to go to hospital but when Dr Stansfield attended, he insisted that the injured man be taken to the Royal Berkshire Hospital for urgent treatment. Annie was taken to the same hospital in the Chief Constable's car but later was told to go back to the shop and come back at 10.00pm when the medical team would know more. By the time she got back to Cross Street, she found that the police had tidied the scene but it was then she checked the till, kept beneath the shop counter, and found that all the notes were missing.

Normally, a piece of card rested in the till, used to separate the ten shilling and one pound notes. That piece of card had been removed from the till, presumably with all the notes, and then discarded onto the shop counter, after the notes had been stolen. When Anne lifted the card, she found a half-crown piece beneath it.

Meanwhile, back at the hospital, Constable William Charles Parfitt had been left with Alfred. At one stage, Alfred said to the constable: 'I was in the room behind the counter when Mrs Oliver went out to Well Street, leaving me to clear away the tea. I had an attache case on the table, containing about thirty pounds in notes and silver, which I last saw just before tea, when I got some change for a man. I think he was from the gas office.' Later still, at around 9.00pm, Alfred was able to add that he had been sitting in the shop, reading a book, at six o'clock or five minutes past. He could recall the name of the book, *A Day from London to Penzance*, but could not remember when, how, or by whom he had been attacked.

At 10.30pm that same evening, 22 June, Dr James Leonard Joyce operated on Alfred, in order to clean up the head wound. Alfred then spent a quiet night in hospital and was conscious on the morning of Sunday 23 June. That evening, however, at 6.00pm, almost exactly twenty-four hours after he had been attacked, Alfred Oliver died from his injuries. The police were now investigating a case of murder.

It was obvious that this might prove to be a difficult case to solve so, on the same day that Alfred Oliver died, the Chief Constable requested assistance from Scotland Yard. That plea resulted in Chief Inspector James Berrett and Detective Sergeant John Harris being despatched to Reading, from London. The two officers arrived at the murder scene on the evening of 23 June.

By the time Berrett and Harris arrived at 15 Cross Street, all the bloodstains had been cleaned up. However, the two officers made a thorough inspection of the premises.

Berrett noted that the shop counter was nine feet six inches long, three feet high and two feet six inches wide. It formed a well between the shop and the dining room at the rear and stood out some two and a half feet from the stock shelves.

The shop window was enclosed by a wooden partition which meant that the space between that and the end of the counter was such that only one person could be there at any time. If, as had been explained, Alfred Oliver positioned his chair at that point, then that chair would have to be moved in order to allow anyone to pass in to the space behind the counter.

The position of the blood splashes on the stock shelves indicated that Alfred had been standing between two showcases when he was attacked. Berrett came to the conclusion that Alfred had been struck from in front. This seemed to be confirmed by the fact that there were blood splashes on a mat in front of the counter, and the finding of the book Alfred had been reading, underneath the counter, open at the page he had reached. The implication was that Alfred Oliver had been sitting in the chair when a customer came in. He stood to attend to that customer, putting his book beneath the counter. He was then attacked. The scales were knocked onto the floor and broken during that attack and the assailant then grabbed the money from the till.

No sooner had the police investigation begun that it seemed that a solution had been reached. At 4.30pm on Monday 24 June, Owen Roberts, a sixty-one-year-old tailor of no fixed abode, walked into Pangbourne police station and admitted that he was responsible for the murder in Reading. He then made a full written statement to the police, which was so filled with inaccuracies and invention that he was obviously inventing the story. Roberts claimed, amongst other things, that he had committed the crime at 9.30pm, and the man he had attacked had a beard. Roberts, in fact, was drunk and once he had sobered up, admitted that none of what he had said was true. The police, rather kindly, released Roberts and put him on a bus home.

The inquest on the dead man opened at 2.45pm, on Tuesday 25 June, before the Borough Coroner, Mr John Lancelot Martin. Only two witnesses were called. Evidence of identity was given by Mr Arthur William Crouch, Nellie Oliver's brother. He was followed to the stand by Dr Joyce who had performed the post-mortem. He described thirteen lacerations on the dead man's scalp, and three large depressed fractures of the skull. The cause of death was those multiple fractures and severe cerebral contusions. The wounds had been caused by a blunt instrument and were consistent with the use of a hammer, a spanner, a jemmy or some other heavy metal object.

Before the proceedings were adjourned, the coroner issued an appeal to anyone who could assist the police in their inquiries, to come forward without delay. He specifically asked for motorists to come forward, who might have given a lift to someone with bloodstained clothing.

In the days after the inquest had closed, two pieces of information came into the hands of Chief Inspector Berrett. The first snippet came from Percy Taylor, who lived at 160 Friar Street. He told the police that he had given Alfred Oliver a cheque, for £1, at 1.45pm on the day of the murder. No trace of this cheque had been found and it was assumed that the person who took the banknotes from the till might also have taken the cheque. True, that cheque might been thrown away afterwards but Barclays Bank were asked to keep an eye out for it in the clearing system. The other piece of information was that a young man had been inside the shop at the approximate time of the murder.

George Charles Jeffries' name had been given to the police as a man suspected of having hit his sister over the head with a jemmy. He had also been seen near the shop, at the relevant time. Jeffries was questioned and admitted that he had been in the shop a minute or two before 6.10pm on the day Alfred had been attacked. He had gone in to buy some cigarettes but there seemed to be no-one there to serve him. He had had a half-crown in his hand, and after waiting for a minute or so, he knocked on the counter to attract someone's attention.

Hearing a noise, Jeffries looked over and saw Mr Oliver lying on the floor in a pool of blood. He immediately ran out of the shop, without reporting what he had seen, and went home. Once there, he told his mother, Emily, what he had seen but said he was too frightened to go to the police.

On the evening of 25 June, the same day that the inquest had been opened and closed, Jeffries finally told his story to Chief Inspector Berrett, explaining that there was another reason he had not come forward. At the time, his sister was critically ill in hospital and Jeffries had been very worried about her. For the time being at least, his story was accepted.

Two days later, on 27 June, Alfred Oliver was laid to rest in Reading Cemetery after a service at All Saints' Church, Downshire Square, conducted by the Reverend George Edwin Jenkins.

The investigation continued and over a period of days, a number of witnesses came forward to describe a man in a blue suit, seen in and around Cross Street on the day of the murder.

William George Loxton was a butcher trading from premises at 19 Cross Street, Reading. He had seen Mr Oliver at around 9.00am on the day of the attack. Later that same day, at round 1.30pm, a man came in and asked William for some calves liver but then didn't wait to be served and headed off in the direction of Friar Street. The man had an accent and later still, at about 6.00pm, William had seen the man again, in Bradley's, which was opposite Alfred Oliver's shop.

William happened to be looking out of his window and saw the man leave Bradley's and head for his butcher's shop. Then, suddenly, the man changed direction and headed off towards Oliver's tobacconists. It would then be about 6.00pm. Soon after this, Nellie Taylor came in and took Constable Chandler across to the scene of the attack.

According to William Loxton, the man he had seen was about five feet eight inches tall. He had dark hair, a sallow complexion, a full clean-shaven face and long, dishevelled hair. He wore a navy blue suit, with brown shoes and a collar and tie. As for the accent William had heard, that might have been American.

Thomas Harold Windle was a sanitary inspector, but on the day of the attack, he had been in Reading with his wife and child. Thomas had arranged to meet his brother and walked up and down Cross Street whilst he was waiting. During that time he saw a man behaving rather oddly. Thomas assumed the man had been drinking as he was looking into various shop windows and mumbling to himself. The man had a raincoat draped over his shoulders like a cape and Thomas watched as he went into the Welcome Café. He described the man as five feet eight inches tall, with a full, red, rather swarthy face and wearing a dark coloured suit. This all took place at around 4.40pm.

Kathleen Earl had also seen a man she described as being drunk, in Cross Street. He was walking in the middle of the road, muttering to himself. It was then around 5.30pm. She went into Loxton's butcher's shop, and when she came out, the man was at the end of Cross Street, close to the junction with Broad Street.

Dorothy Gladys Irene Shepherd was also in Cross Street on 22 June and her evidence might prove to be of crucial importance. She was looking into a shop window at around 6.15pm when she saw a man running out of Alfred Oliver's shop. He ran off towards Friar Street but she didn't see the man's face. He was wearing a navy blue serge suit.

The most important witness of all, however, was probably Mrs Alice James. She had also been in Reading town centre on 22 June. At around 6.10pm she passed Oliver's tobacconist's shop. There were very few people around at the time and, as she passed the shop, she saw a man standing inside the doorway, wiping blood from his face. The man was fairly tall, quite stout and wore dark clothing. Alice estimated his age as somewhere between forty and fifty. He wore no hat or glasses and had dishevelled hair. Shown a photograph of the dead man, Alice swore that this was not the man she had seen in the doorway.

Over the next few weeks, a number of what proved to be false leads, came into the hands of the police. Thus, for example, Frederick Charles Miles contacted the police at Twickenham, saying that he had been speaking to a man named Sidney Walter Coe who claimed to know who had committed the crime. When Coe was interviewed he told a story of three knife-grinders who had no money before the murder, but lots of it afterwards. A check on Coe's background soon showed that his story was an invention and as for Miles, the man who had first gone to the police, he had been a recent inmate of a mental hospital.

As June turned into July, the investigation slowed to a halt and little new information came in. Then, purely by chance, the name of a prime suspect was given to the Chief Constable himself.

A description of the mysterious man, seen by a number of people in Cross Street, had been published in all the local newspapers. On 19 July, almost a month after the crime had been committed, Chief Constable Burrows was in the Wellington Club in Friar Street, when a fellow member

Philip Yale Drew, who was suspected of the murder. This picture is taken from his identity card. The National Archives

Another picture of Drew, in his guise as Young Buffalo. This picture is also taken from his identity card. The National Archives

approached him and said that the description matched an actor who had recently appeared at the Royal County Theatre in a play entitled *The Monster*. Further, the informant could put a name to the actor. He was an American named Philip Yale Drew.

Philip Drew had had quite a successful career in the United States. He had made a number of films, most of them Westerns, where he played the role of Young Buffalo. An accomplished actor, he had been in England a number of years but his fondness for drink meant that his career was now rather slowing down and he now took fairly minor stage roles.

A quick police check showed that Drew had arrived in Reading on 16 June 1929, and lodged at 9 King's Meadow. He had left the town on Sunday 23 June, the day after the attack upon Alfred Oliver and further checks showed that the theatrical company he was a member of was now in St Helens but would, on 22 July, move on to Nottingham.

On 23 July, confirmation came from the police at Nottingham that the play's company had duly arrived in the city and that Drew was still a member of the cast. The following day, 24 July, Detective Sergeant Harris and Chief Constable Burrows, drove down to Nottingham. That same night, an officer followed Drew from the theatre, after his performance, and noted that he was now lodging at 37 Fox Road, West Bridgford. The next morning, Thursday 25 July, three officers, including Sergeant Harris, called on Drew at his lodgings and took him to the police station to be interviewed.

The interview lasted for around three hours before Drew was allowed to leave. He performed, as usual, on stage that evening and the next day, 26 July, he was interviewed for a second time. Whilst that interview was taking place, officers collected a blue serge jacket which Drew had left at a cleaner's in Nottingham. That same evening, Sergeant Harris returned to Reading, taking the jacket with him for examination. In fact, no trace of blood was ever found on the garment, though it had already been cleaned.

The theatre company left Nottingham and moved on to Bolton, where they arrived on 29 July. From there they moved on again, on 4 August, to St Albans. It was there, on 7 August, that Drew was interviewed for a third time. It was by now clear that Drew was the chief suspect, at least as far as the police were concerned, and eventually it was decided that Drew should return to Reading, as an important witness at the reconvened inquest.

The adjourned inquest reopened on Wednesday 2 October 1929, with Mr Martin once more in charge. The first two witnesses were the two gentlemen who had given evidence at the first hearing. First, Arthur Crouch repeated his evidence of identification and then Dr Joyce detailed the injuries Alfred Oliver had suffered.

The first new witness was Annie Oliver, the dead man's wife. She said again that she had served six customers, all men, whilst her husband was clearing away the tea things. She then took the dog outside, not returning to the shop until 6.15pm. Since she had left the shop at around 6.05pm, the attack must have taken place within that gap of ten minutes.

Afterwards a number of police witnesses gave evidence, including Chief Inspector Harry Battley, of the fingerprint bureau. He had discovered a bloodstained imprint on a showcase inside the shop, which police had first belived had come from the killer, but tests had shown that this belonged to George Taylor, who had come into the shop to give assistance after Alfred had been injured.

In fact, this point illustrated just how foolish part of the investigation had been. During Drew's interview, a piece of blank paper had been left in the room whilst Drew was alone. The hope was that he would, out of curiosity, pick the paper up, leave behind his prints and that these would then be checked against the bloody imprint found at the scene.

Twenty-one-year-old George Jeffries, and his mother, Emily, were the next two witnesses. He repeated his story of seeing

Alfred injured in the shop, but being too frightened to report it. His mother said that when he returned home he was very frightened and had changed his clothes but swore that there were no stains of any kind on the items he had removed.

The witnesses who had seen the strange man in and around Cross Street were then called. William Loxton spoke of the man with the accent who had come into his shop. However, when asked if he could see the man in court, Loxton pointed to Drew and said that he was certain that he was the man. The first identification of Philip Drew had been made. At that point, the inquest was adjourned until the following day.

On 3 October, the second day of the inquest, another positive identification of Philip Drew followed. The first witness, Alice James, swore that the man she had seen wiping blood from his face was none other than Drew. She was followed to the stand by Charles Russell, the stage-manager at the theatre.

Charles said that on 22 June, at around 1.30pm, he had gone for a drink with Drew in Friar Street. Some fifteen minutes later, Drew had said that he was going to Cross Street to buy a newspaper. It was known that the shop next door to the murder scene, was a newsagents. This was confirmed by Harry George Ingram, and James Henry Grubb who also worked at the theatre and who had gone with Russell and Drew to Friar Street. They too had heard Drew say he was going to Cross Street.

The next witness was Thomas Windle who told his story of the man he had seen in Cross Street. He also positively identified Drew as the man he had observed. He was followed by Nellie Taylor of the Welcome Café, who now recalled Drew as a customer who had eaten four fried eggs, two rashers of bacon, bread and butter and black coffee on either 18 or 19 June. She had seen him again on 22 June, at some time between 4.15pm and 4.30pm.

Other witnesses also identified Drew. Sydney Eric Turnbull, an estate agent, had seen a man behaving suspiciously in Cross

Street on the day of the murder. He too pointed out Drew as the man he had seen.

Kathleen Earl positively identified Drew as the man with the reddish face, who she had seen walking in the middle of the road and muttering to himself.

George Thomas Nicholson was a gardener but he had been in Cross Street at around 5.20pm. He had actually gone into Alfred Oliver's shop to buy some cigarettes. Alfred had come through from the room at the back in order to serve him. There was no-one else in the shop at the time but when George left, he stood outside for a time, waiting for his wife. A man came from the direction of Broad Street. He appeared to be drunk. For once, however, Drew was not picked out as the man who had been seen.

Things were looking decidedly bad for Philip Yale Drew. A number of witnesses had testified that he had said he was going to Cross Street to buy a newspaper and then others had put him in that street at about the time the murder took place. Indeed one, Alice James, had actually put him in the doorway of Mr Oliver's shop, wiping blood from his face.

The next witness was Marion Lindo, the owner of the theatre company, of which Drew was a member. She told the court that whilst the company was in Reading, she and her husband, Frank, had stayed at 77 Vastern Road. Although Drew had lodged at a different address, in King's Meadow Road, this was very close to Vastern Road and he had had all his meals, except for breakfast, with them.

On 22 June 1929, the day Alfred Oliver had been attacked in his shop, Drew had had lunch with the Lindos, at some time between 2.00pm and 2.30pm. Marion went on to say that Drew appeared somewhat flushed and she believed that he might have been drinking. Drew, it seems, had a drink problem and sometimes this had even affected his performance on stage. This concerned Marion and she tried to look after Drew and prevent him from drinking too much.

On this particular day, Frank Lindo advised Drew that he should have a nap after they had finished lunch. Drew lay on a settee and went to sleep and it was Marion who woke him, at around 4.00pm. As Drew rose, Marion noticed a shape in his pocket, which looked to her like a small bottle of whisky. She demanded that he hand the bottle over but Drew would have none of it. He flatly denied that it was a bottle of whisky and refused to empty his pockets.

A brief argument followed and Drew went back to his own lodgings. Marion followed him there later and last saw him at 5.00pm, after telling him not to bother coming to the theatre that night if he was drunk. That evening, she was in her dressing-room at the theatre when she heard Drew, who had the next room, come in a few minutes before 6.20pm. She was able to narrow the time down so accurately as it was just before the half-hour call before curtain up, which was at 6.50pm.

Marion Lindo's evidence was important because it contradicted all those who claimed to have seen Drew in Cross Street on the afternoon of 22 June. Marion had indicated that he could not have been in Cross Street any earlier than say 5.10pm. It did not, however, give him an alibi for the actual time of the attack upon Alfred Oliver.

Alfred George Fry was one of the stage-managers for the theatre company and he testified that on 22 June he had been drinking with Drew, in the *Marquis of Lorne*, before 2.00pm. Drew had been drinking ginger ale. The two men left the public house at closing time and Drew said he was going to have lunch with the Lindos. That evening, Fry was at the theatre by 5.45pm. He said that it was closer to 6.00pm when Drew arrived. Though Fry didn't see him, he did hear Drew singing so was sure that it was him. Fry actually saw Drew at 6.17pm, standing at his dressing-room door. He had changed into his costume for the evening performance but had not, as yet, applied his make-up.

By all accounts, Alfred Oliver had been attacked within a

minute or two of 6.10pm. If Fry's testimony was accurate, then Drew could not be the murderer as he was at the theatre by close on 6.00pm.

The next witness was Mrs Mary Eleanor Goodall. She lived at 9 King's Meadow and had been Drew's landlady whilst he was staying in Reading. She began by confirming that Drew had stayed at her house from 16 June until 23 June. On 22 June, he had left her house at 11.00am and returned, after lunch, at some time between 3.00pm and 3.30pm. Shortly afterwards, Marion Lindo arrived and told Mary that she and Drew had argued over a bottle of whisky he was carrying. As the two women talked, Drew came downstairs and went out. It was then around 5.00pm and he was back by 5.15pm. He stayed at the house until about 6.10pm. Mary remembered the time because she told Drew he would be late if he didn't get a move on. He replied that he could walk to the theatre in seven minutes.

Under cross-examination, Mary had to agree that although there were many clocks in her house, none of them were set to the correct time so she was therefore unable to say, with

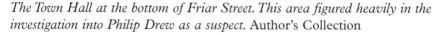

The Town Hall at the bottom of Friar Street. This area figured heavily in the investigation into Philip Drew as a suspect. Author's Collection

accuracy, that it was indeed 6.10pm when Drew left her house to go to the theatre.

The next two witnesses were, however, able to narrow down the time Drew had left for the theatre. Elizabeth Crouch also lived in King's Meadow, at number 16, and on 22 June, she and her husband were walking home from the town centre. They passed the Town Hall at some time between 6.05pm and 6.10pm and, as they arrived at King's Meadow, they saw Drew rushing out of number 9. By Mrs Crouch's estimation, it would then be approximately 6.10pm.

Drew dashing out of his lodgings was also seen by Mrs Winifred Greenwood, who lived next door at number 7. She could not be precisely sure of the time but said it would be around 6.00pm.

All of these witnesses, if accurate, indicated that there was no way Drew could have been the man who attacked Mr Oliver at around 6.10pm. Just as it seemed that there might be hope for Drew, another witness appeared to put things in doubt once again.

Bertie Hathaway was a one-legged man, who could only walk with the aid of a crutch. He testified that at 6.00pm on 22 June, he was standing outside a music shop on Friar Street, talking to a lady named Mrs Williams. They parted after about five or six minutes and Hathaway then travelled down Friar Street, towards the theatre. As he approached Queen Victoria Street he saw a powerfully built man, muttering to himself, almost pushing people out of the way, and also heading towards the theatre. At one stage, a passing bus held up both Hathaway and the man and the latter cursed at it.

This strange behaviour caused Hathaway to observe the man, as he went on his way, and Hathaway saw him turn into the theatre itself. Hathaway then asked an attendant who the man was, but he had been unable to say. Hathaway, however, was now able to say that the man was in court, was none other than Drew, and his entrance to the theatre had been at 6.15pm.

Once again, there was doubt. If the timings of those who had seen Drew leave his lodgings were just a few minutes out, then Drew could have been in Cross Street by around 6.00pm, could have struck down Alfred Oliver at around 6.10pm, and could have been seen by Hathaway, hurrying from the scene, towards the theatre, shortly afterwards.

The next few witnesses were all serving police officers. Detective Sergeant Percy Richard Ellington, of the Nottingham City Police, told of going to Drew's lodgings in West Bridgford and asking him to come to the police station for interview.

He was followed into the witness box by Detective Sergeant John Harris who gave details of Drew's statement in which he denied even knowing of Cross Street, and had not even heard of the murder there until after his company left the town. Harris then detailed Drew's second statement, given after he had been told that a number of witnesses had now identified him as being in Cross Street on 22 June. He merely said, again, that he had not been in Cross Street and had not been into Mr Oliver's tobacconists at any time.

On the afternoon of the fifth day of the hearing, Philip Yale Drew stepped into the witness box to tell his own story. Under questioning he admitted that he did like a drink but denied ever being 'falling down drunk'. Turning to the events of 22 June, he claimed to have little memory of exact times and places but did remember being in the theatre at his usual time, which would be approximately one hour before curtain up; that is, by about 5.50pm. Drew went on to deny that he had ever said that he was going to Cross Street to buy a newspaper. He admitted that he may have said that was going across the street, to get a paper from the newsagents opposite the theatre, and that might have been misheard. He had not been in Cross Street at any time and was not responsible for Mr Oliver's death.

The final day of testimony was Wednesday 9 October 1929. By now, public opinion had swung directly behind Philip Drew.

There may have been a feeling that the man had not been treated properly by either the police or the authorities, or that the evidence against him was purely circumstantial, but crowds lined the streets as Drew and his supporters made their way to the courtroom. Many shouted messages of support, other thrust flowers into his hands.

During the morning, Drew continued his own testimony. That afternoon, Mr Frank Lindo gave evidence about Drew's drinking but he was unable to narrow down the time of Drew's arrival at the theatre on 22 June, as Lindo had gone to the cinema that afternoon and had not arrived at the theatre himself until well after 6.00pm. Then, finally, the last witness was called.

Alfred John Wells was a butcher's assistant and worked at 22 Cross Street. On 22 June, he had seen a strange man, in Cross Street, on a number of occasions.

The first time had been at 7.30am, in the Welcome Café. The man was about five feet ten inches tall, long dark hair, and wore a blue coat, a blue waistcoat, grey trousers and brown shoes. Wells had heard the man speak, and said that he had a North Country accent.

Later that same day, Wells was wiping down the window of the butcher's shop where he worked when he saw the same man again. In fact, he saw him two or three times, the final time being at about 5.40pm when the man was walking from Cross Street into Friar Street. Asked if he could identify Drew as this man, Wells stated that he was absolutely certain that he was not.

Perhaps of even more importance was the way the police had treated Mr Wells after the news of the murder had become public. Wells had known of the attack upon Alfred Oliver even before the injured man was taken out of his shop. Wells had then gone to a policeman and told him of the strange man he had seen and was told to go to the police station to make a report. Wells had gone to the station that same evening, at about 9.00pm and made a statement to a police sergeant. He did not know the officer's name but, by coincidence, Wells had seen

The crowds gathered in support of Drew at the end of the inquest. Drew and some of his closest supporters are on the balcony to the top left of the picture. Author's Collection

that same officer outside the court, helping to control the crowd of Drew's supporters.

The officer, Sergeant Arthur Colbert, was brought into court and claimed to have no memory of taking a statement from Mr Wells. However, the defence team then produced the statement and asked Sergeant Colbert to read it out. It agreed completely with the testimony Wells had just given in court.

On 10 October, the coroner summed up the evidence for the jury. They retired to consider their verdict and when it came, it was that the evidence was too conflicting for them to establish the guilt of any individual. The verdict was that Alfred Oliver, had been murdered by some person or persons unknown.

Just as it seemed that the entire matter might fall from public consciousness, yet another remarkable coincidence occurred in the affair. Just over two weeks after the inquest had closed, the police received news that not one, but two separate confessions had been received.

On 27 October 1929, two men both said that they had been responsible for the murder of Alfred Oliver. In Glasgow, a man named Philip Joseph Dickens, said that he was guilty and, on the same date, Joseph Cassidy had made a similar claim, in London.

Dickens had walked into the Central Police Station in Glasgow at 2.20pm and said that he wished to confess to the murder of Alfred Oliver, in Reading. He went on to make a full written statement in which he said he had been at Kingston-upon-Thames, on 21 June, with two friends; Ernie Carter and James Maguire. Carter lived in Reading and they all arranged to meet up at his house the following day. On 22 June, Dickens arrived at Reading between 6.30am and 7.30am and asked a policeman for directions to Carter's home. Dickens claimed that at the time, he was carrying a railway spike, which he had picked up on his journey.

Later that same day, Dickens had met up with Maguire, who told him about a tobacconist's shop where the owner kept fifty or sixty pounds in a drawer underneath the shop counter. Dickens had then gone to the shop, hit Oliver with the iron spike and taken the money from the till. He had then thrown the spike onto some allotments, along with a handkerchief, before travelling on to London.

At first, it appeared that there might be some substance to Dickens' claim. There were allotments along the direct route Dickens would have taken on his journey to London. They were searched and an iron railway spike, and a handkerchief, which looked as if it might be bloodstained, were discovered.

The police believed they might have a strong case against Dickens and he was taken to Reading for further questioning. Unfortunately, in the meantime, other railway spikes were found on those same allotments and none could be shown to be the murder weapon.

Further disappointments were to follow for the police. Dickens was a married man and his wife was able to prove that he had not been out of Glasgow since March 1929. He had enjoyed a brief holiday but that was in September, long after Alfred Oliver was dead. This evidence was confirmed by Dickens' son, Joseph, and a neighbour, Mrs Elizabeth Patterson, who had visited the family many times in June, during which, Dickens had always been there. As if that were not enough, Dickens had even visited his own family doctor on 22 June.

Joseph Cassidy had also walked into a police station, this time on Blackheath Road, in London, and confessed to the crime. Enquiries were made by Detective Inspector Rakey, who was able to prove that Cassidy had never set foot in Reading. Cassidy was diagnosed as being a manic depressive and was taken to the Greenwich and Deptford Institute, for observation. By yet another remarkable coincidence, it was revealed that both Dickens and Cassidy, men who had confessed at opposite ends of the country, on the same day, had once both been inmates of the Ewell Hospital.

The year 1929 passed and the murder of Alfred Oliver remained unsolved. Anne Elizabeth Oliver, the murdered man's wife, sold the shop before the end of the year.

There were still those, especially perhaps amongst the ranks of the police, who believed that Philip Yale Drew was indeed guilty of the murder, but the vast majority of people believed that justice had been served.

The investigation had closed. The inquest was over, the verdict was an open one and no charges were ever placed against Drew, or indeed any other individual. Other confessions were made over the next few years but all proved to be groundless and the murder of Alfred Oliver remains unsolved to this day.

The publicity surrounding the case damaged Drew's career beyond repair, and over the next few years he had very little work indeed. At one stage, he was even forced to sell newspapers, outside the theatres he loved so much, in order to make ends meet. Drew's health deteriorated and he died, from throat cancer, in the Lambeth Hospital, on 2 July 1940. He was sixty years old.

CHAPTER 7

Too Good to Live
Queenie Pennington
1929

By 1929, William Pennington and his wife, Queenie, had been married for four years, and their union had been blessed, in June 1926, with a daughter who they named Jean. The problem was, however, that this did not bring the couple closer together as might be expected, for Queenie began to suffer from depression.

William worked as a roadman, for Berkshire Council and, on the morning of Friday 30 August 1929, left for work, as usual, at 6.30am. He did not return to his home at 2 Fairview Cottages, Amen Corner, Binfield, until 5.05pm, and when he did he found that the door was locked against him.

William knocked on the door a number of times and, finally, saw that the scullery door was opening. He dashed forward, only to find his wife in the doorway with a vicious gash in her throat. William ran for a neighbour and asked him to call the doctor before he went back into his house. Going inside, William found, to his horror, that his daughter Jean lay on the scullery floor, in a pool of blood, her head almost severed from her body.

The first police officer to arrive was Constable Thatcher, who knew the family well. He took a note of the position of

Jean's body and also that the child was still warm, showing that the crime had only taken place very recently. Queenie was now lying on the floor, next to her daughter, unconscious. A check of the premises revealed a razor in the sink and a hammer on the floor, both of which were heavily bloodstained. There was also a good deal of blood on the scullery floor and in the kitchen.

At 5.20pm, Dr Lancelot George Jacobs arrived. He determined that Jean's throat had been cut very deeply and her windpipe severed. He then administered medical aid to Queenie, before she was taken to the Guardian's Institution at Easthampstead. The body of the child was taken to the mortuary at the same establishment and the following day, 31 August, Dr Jacobs carried out a post-mortem.

That examination showed that there were a number of brown stains on the child's hands and lips. There were similar stains on the side of Jean's head and also on her legs. The doctor concluded that these had probably been caused by someone trying to force some kind of liquid into the child's mouth, and the consequent movements as Jean struggled against it. Finally, Dr Jacobs was able to put the time of death at some twenty to thirty minutes before his initial examination, or close to ten minutes to five.

The inquest on Jean Pennington opened on Monday 2 September, before Mr R S Payne, the coroner for East Berkshire. Evidence of identification was given by Constable Thatcher and details of the cause of death were outlined by Dr Jacobs. The proceedings were then adjourned until 7 October, by which time it was hoped that Queenie might have recovered sufficiently from her injuries.

In fact, Queenie Pennington made a reasonably rapid recovery and, by 10 September, was well enough to attend a magistrates' hearing. Queenie, wearing a blue suit, and with her throat heavily bandaged, sat motionless in the dock throughout.

Ellen May Haines lived in the front two rooms at the house where the Penningtons resided and she told the court that she had seen the baby alive and well at approximately 3.00pm on the fateful day. Mrs Haines also testified that in her opinion, Queenie had seemed to be devoted to her daughter.

Margaret Smedley was a district nurse and she had been called to the scene to attend to Queenie. By the time she arrived, Queenie had been assisted into a chair. After she had dressed Queenie's throat wound, Margaret had noticed an envelope on the kitchen table. This, it transpired, was a note which read: 'I can't stand living any longer. Please take this as the truth from me. I am only blaming myself.' The note was signed: 'Mrs Pennington'.

The brown stains found on Jean had also been noted on Queenie's lips. This was almost certainly Potassium Permanganate. When he had searched the premises, Constable Thatcher had found a half-used packet of that chemical on the kitchen shelf. It was possible that Queenie had tried to poison her daughter and herself, before turning to the razor.

Superintendent Goddard had questioned Queenie, once she had recovered sufficiently from her injuries. She had explained to him that she had intended to kill herself, not Jean, and could not remember why she had cut her daughter's throat. She went on to say: 'I have always suffered with my head. I really didn't mean to kill Jean; it was myself I wished to kill. I could not put up with the pain any more.'

Queenie Pennington was duly committed for trial on the charge of murder. In the event, Queenie stood in the dock at Reading on 14 October, before Mr Justice Acton. Mr HH Maddocks led the case for the Crown whilst Queenie was defended by Mr St John G Micklethwait. She pleaded not guilty to the charge.

The events inside 2 Fairview Cottages were then reconstructed. Prior to the crime, Queenie had seemed to live happily with her husband and daughter, to whom she was, undoubtedly, devoted. However, at some time between 4.45pm and 5.15pm on 30 August, she had first tried to get Jean to drink Potassium Permanganate, and when this failed, she had then cut Jean's throat with her husband's razor and then turned the weapon upon herself. When these efforts did not succeed in ending her life, she had then taken a hammer and struck herself repeatedly over the head. There was no motive for the crime and the defence were therefore claiming that, at the time she committed this crime, Queenie had been insane.

Dr Jacobs, in addition to repeating his medical testimony, was also able to say that whilst he and William Pennington had been alone with Queenie, she had said: 'The child was too good to live.'

Ellen Haines testified that Queenie had been very much 'up and down' before 30 August. She was easily excited and sometimes seemed to suffer from bouts of melancholia.

Constable Thatcher, in addition to his evidence already detailed, pointed out to the court that no attempt had been made to conceal Jean's body, as might have been expected in a case of wilful murder.

The final witness was Dr John Hall Morton, the senior medical officer at Holloway prison, where Queenie had been held. He had observed her since her reception there on 14 September and reported that she appeared depressed and dull. She had difficulty in holding a normal conversation and, in his opinion, was suffering from some mental abnormaility.

On 26 September, Queenie had complained to Dr Morton of severe pains in her head. Later still she had a violent outburst and tried to ram her head against the wall. In Dr Morton's opinion, Queenie knew what she had done to her daughter but had no concept of it being wrong. His opinion was that she was certainly insane at the time of the attack.

Having heard all the evidence, the jury reached their verdict without even leaving the courtroom. Queenie was guilty, but insane. She was then sentenced to be detained as a criminal lunatic until His Majesty's pleasure be known.

Queenie Pennington was granted one last request. Before she was taken away, the judge allowed her to see her husband, William, the man who had come home from work and found his family destroyed.

CHAPTER 8

Behind Closed Doors
Ernest Hutchinson
1932

There was something very curious going on in the house at 8 Heywood Avenue, White Waltham, near Maidenhead. Joseph Thomas Hutton, a retired policeman who lived next door at number 9, had been watching the various comings and goings with great interest.

The house at number 8 was occupied by four people. As far as Mr Hutton knew, these were Gwendoline Annie Warren, her husband Ernest and their two children: twelve-year-old Ronald Jeffrey and the baby, Connie. In fact, things were more complex than that, for Mr and Mrs Warren were not man and wife and Ernest Warren's real name was actually Ernest Hutchinson.

Mr Hutton had last seen Mrs Warren at around 9.15pm on Saturday 10 September 1932. The following day, Sunday 11, at 11.00am, Hutton saw Ernest Hutchinson and remarked that he hadn't seen Gwendoline up and about as yet. Hutchinson told him that she was still in bed, to which Joseph Hutton said that she must be making a day of it then. Hutchinson agreed and the matter was left there.

Joseph Hutton saw Hutchinson again the following morning, at 9.00am. Once again he asked after Mrs Warren and was told that she had gone to Birmingham and would be there until the following Tuesday. He said he was finding it rather difficult to look after two children, so added that he intended taking them to Burnham, in Buckinghamshire, to stay with relatives there.

At this stage, nothing had really happened to arouse Joseph Hutton's suspicions but then, at 6.00pm on that same Tuesday evening, 13 September, a gentleman called to see Hutchinson at number 8. The very next morning, Wednesday 14 September, a carrier's van with the word 'Bunce' painted on the side, appeared outside number 8 and Mr Hutton saw a piano, a table and a settee loaded onto it. Shortly after this, at 12.15pm, Hutchinson bumped into Mr Hutton and announced that he too was now going to Birmingham, to be with his wife, but would travel via Oxford. He then closed the door behind him, made sure it was locked, and walked off down the street, taking the two children with him. It was now close to 12.30pm on 14 September 1932.

For a few hours at least, Mr Hutton saw nothing more to arouse his curiosity. Then, at around 6.00pm, he saw twelve-year-old Ronald Warren return to the house with a woman Mr Hutton did not recognise. The two visitors were unable to gain access to number 8 despite their constant knocking, and Mr Hutton went to see if he could help in any way.

The woman with Ronald was his aunt, Mrs Mable Ellen Clara Fleet who lived at School House, East Burnham, Buckinghamshire. After Joseph Hutton had introduced himself, he assisted Ronald through the larder window at the rear of the house. Ronald then opened the front door but as soon as Mrs Fleet stepped inside, Mr Hutton called her back out and told her to take care of the boy. His police training told him that there might well be something untoward inside the house and he felt that he should make a search of the premises himself.

The house was tidy enough but when Mr Hutton went into the front bedroom, it became clear that all was not well. A large pile of bedding, weights and other items were tied into a bundle and placed on top of the bed. Beneath this, lay the body of a woman. Mr Hutton wasted no time in calling for the police.

The pile of bedding and weights that was deposited on top of Gwendoline Warren's body. The National Archives

The body of Gwendoline Warren, in situ. The National Archives

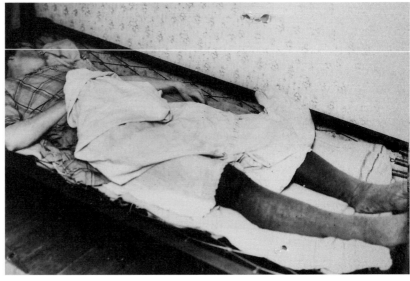

A description of Ernest Hutchinson was circulated and reports of the crime appeared in many local and national newspapers. On Thursday 15 September, those reports were seen by Mrs Jasper, the landlady of a boarding house at 11

Ernest Hutchinson. This newspaper picture was published after the trial was concluded. The National Archives

Broadway Market, Southend-on-Sea, who believed that the description matched a guest who had signed in the previous night. That guest had a woman with him and they had signed the register as Mr and Mrs Hutchinson, giving an address at Haywood Avenue, Buckinghamshire. The similarity of the addresses and the mention of Buckinghamshire were too much for coincidence and Mrs Jasper telephoned the police. At 5.30pm that evening, Detective Inspector WA Harris visited the hotel and took Ernest Hutchinson into custody.

Told that he was being held on a charge of murder, Hutchinson claimed that he had nothing to do with the crime. According to his statement, he and Gwendoline had argued on the night of Saturday 10 September and, as a result, she had gone to sleep alone in the front bedroom. The following morning he went to check on her and found that she was dead. The front door had been left unlocked and it was plain that someone had entered the house and killed Gwendoline. In fact, Hutchinson was even able to supply the police with the name of a suspect: Gwendoline's estranged husband, Thomas, who had been writing her threatening letters.

Hutchinson admitted that he had not reported this to the authorities and had stayed in the house with the body for a few days but that did not make him guilty of murder. The police believed none of this story and Hutchinson was then formally charged.

Forty-three-year-old Ernest Hutchinson appeared at Reading before Mr Justice MacKinnon on 14 October 1932. During the two-day trial, the case for the Crown was led by Mr WG Earengey whilst Hutchinson was defended by Mr St John G Micklethwait.

One of the early witnesses was Thomas William Warren who testified that he had married Gwendoline Annie Fleet, in Reigate, on 8 March 1924. They had lived happily enough for a time but then, on 5 July 1930, Hutchinson had come to live with them as a lodger. That same night, Gwendoline had run away with Hutchinson, taking Ronald with them. It was true that they had returned the next day, but things were never the same after that, even when Hutchinson went away for the best part of two years. Eventually, Hutchinson returned and soon afterwards, Gwendoline fell pregnant. This was not Thomas' child. Then, some three months before she had died, Gwendoline had left again, with Hutchinson, taking the children with them. Thomas denied that he had sent any threatening letters to his wife and, in fact, had only communicated with her once or twice since that final separation, to discuss the possibility of a divorce.

Continuing his evidence, Thomas Warren gave details of a letter he had received from Gwendoline, which seemed to throw some light on a possible motive for the crime. Dated 10 September, the most probable date of Gwendoline's death, it began:

Dear Tom, I have found out my mistake now – wish I had never come down. He has been making out to me, for the last five weeks, that he has been working at the Maidenhead Gas Company and I have partly believed it.

I wrote to the manager yesterday to make sure, and had a reply this morning to say they had nobody in their employ in that name. I have not had a penny from him ever since we have been here, only what he has got somehow, I think from my account at the Post Office.

Ever since last Tuesday he has been saying that he had got £17, which was a month's wages, in his purse and I should have it. He has also entered four weeks rent as paid in the rent book, but I got to know this morning that it has not been paid at all.

Oh Tom, can you forgive me once more and I will not do it again. I will be true to you now and for all time.

I know I should not expect it, nor I know I don't deserve it but will you please stop divorce proceedings and come back to me? I was not happy with you, I know, but we shall have to get along somehow. It does not matter about the neighbours. The people next door one side have been very good. When I got that letter this morning they made me go in and have a cup of tea.

Could you please help me out for the rent next Monday as I have two weeks to pay?

The letter was signed 'Gwen' but Thomas Warren never had a chance to reply to his estranged wife. The very next day a postcard arrived. Dated 11 September and in Hutchinson's hand, it read:

Sorry to trouble you, but Gwen asked me to write and tell you that she withdraws the letter posted Saturday and she has gone to Birmingham until Wednesday next and I am looking after baby and Ron until then, as she has decided to go to Birmingham to live with me again so she is trying to get three rooms while she is there.

The inference was clear. Gwendoline had discovered that Hutchinson had been lying, had no job and no income and had been drawing money from her Post Office account. They had argued and he had killed her and tried to cover his tracks.

Twelve-year-old Ronald Jeffrey Warren told the court of the various trips he had made over those crucial dates. On Saturday 10 September, he had been sent to his aunt's house in East Burnham. The next day he returned to White Waltham at 9.05pm and at first there was no answer to his knocking. Finally, Hutchinson opened the door and when Ronald asked after his mother, Hutchinson replied: 'Your mother is not in. Here is a note that she wrote.'

Hutchinson handed Ronald a scrap of paper on which was written:

> *Dear Ronnie,*
> *I have gone to Birmingham so be a good boy, but daddy will look after Connie and you.*
> *Signed Mummy, with love and kisses.*

Ronald thought nothing more about it, had his supper and went straight to bed. A couple of days later, on Tuesday 13 September, after he had had breakfast, Hutchinson announced that Ronald and Connie were going to his aunt's house in East Burnham. Later that day, all three of them got onto a bus, which took them to Maidenhead. From there, they caught another bus to Slough and then Hutchinson put the two children on a third bus to Farnham Common, asking the conductor if he would put them off there. Once he arrived, Ronald walked the rest of the way to his aunt's house.

The next day, Wednesday, Mrs Fleet, his aunt, suggested that Ronald should go back to the house in White Waltham and bring the note Hutchinson had shown him. A somewhat weary Ronald did as he was asked but when he got back to Heywood Avenue, Hutchinson was just coming out of the gate and announced that he was going to Birmingham. They got on the bus together and went to the railway station at Maidenhead, where Ronald heard Hutchinson buy a ticket to Paddington before putting him back on the bus. Ronald was despatched back to his aunt's house and it was then that she decided to return with him.

After Joseph Hutton had given his testimony, his wife, Beatrice Emily Madeline Hutton took the stand and her evidence reinforced what Gwendoline had written in the letter to her husband.

Beatrice detailed a conversation she had had with Gwendoline on the day she was last seen alive. Gwendoline was very upset and explained that all the money had been drawn out of her account at the post office. Further, Hutchinson had lied to her. He had told her that he had a good job but this was simply not true. He had been keeping the household going by drawing the money from her account. So upset was Gwendoline at the time, that Mrs Hutton took her into her own house and made her a cup of tea.

Albert Davies, a dealer, of 38 Bridge Street, Maidenhead, confirmed that Hutchinson had come into his shop and asked him to purchase a piano. A price was agreed and the next morning, Albert made arrangements with William Bunce of 29 Harrow Lane, Maidenhead, to take his van and collect it. Once at Hutchinson's house, Mr Davies also purchased a settee and a table, paying well below the market value for all three items. Hutchinson, it seems, was only interested in raising some cash and did not care what price he received.

One of the final witnesses was Doris Dew, a prostitute of 1 Oakenham Street, Kennington Road, London. She told the court that she had met Hutchinson in the *York Hotel* on Waterloo Road, and after falling into conversation with him, he had suggested that they should go to Southend together. She had agreed and was with him in the hotel when he was arrested.

The jury retired to consider their verdict and, after deliberating for one hour and ten minutes, returned to announce that Hutchinson was guilty as charged. He was then sentenced to death by the trial judge. Hutchinson seemed unperturbed. He smiled as the foreman gave the guilty verdict, when the judge donned the black cap, and as the warders took him down to the cells.

1248 E. Hutchinson (1)   20th November

To Governor Comissioners & Home Secitary.
I Ernest Hutchinson make this statment to all & Public.
I am about to be hung at Oxford Prison on the 23rd Nov
for living with a Woman, who was Murdered, but not
by me, which I swear on my oath. My last words will
be, Not Guilty. The man who hangs me. I hope God will
strike him dead. The truth I told of the Woman's doing's
in my Petition, also at Court, but I am not believed
I admit I told lies about the Woman going to Birmingham as I didnt know what to do. The Furniture was sold
by her permission. The Bank Book business. I swear I
never forged. Never in Bray Post Office in my life. I had
no cause for Mrs Warren never refused me nothing.
I Ernest Hutchinson have been punished now since the
15th Sept until the 23rd Nov. I shall carry on to the last
knowing that on God's honour that my hands are free
from Murder which I swear before God & the whole
World. Sir Goveror & I ask you this Favour befor I
go which I want Registered to Home Office at my
own exspence. Signed Ernest Hutchinson
       Not Guilty of the
       Charge alleged

       Hutchinson E.

Recievd from prisoner 9.45 am.
20.11.32.

A letter, written by Hutchinson after his conviction, protesting his innocence.
The National Archives

Only now could some of Hutchinson's past be detailed. He had been born at Christchurch in 1891 and had first come to the attention of the police in 1910 when he was sentenced to five months in prison for stealing a postal packet whilst employed by the Royal Mail.

Since that date he had received no fewer than sixteen prison sentences, only finally being discharged on 7 June 1932, from a two year sentence for false pretences. He had appeared before Canterbury magistrates on 6 October 1930. In fact, he had spent very little time outside of jail between 1910 and 1932.

An appeal was entered, the three grounds given were, that the prosecution had failed to provide any motive for the alleged offence; that the verdict was against the weight of evidence; and that Hutchinson was simply not guilty of murder. The appeal was dismissed as being worthless and the sentence was confirmed. Finally, on Wednesday 23 November 1932, Ernest Hutchinson was hanged at Oxford.

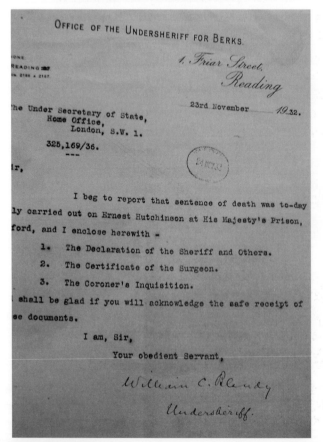

Ernest Hutchinson's death notice from Oxford prison. The National Archives

CHAPTER 9

The Airman
Eric Stanley Pocock
1946

onstable Ronald John George Haunton was having a quiet enough night on Sunday 1 September 1946, when his beat took him into Friar Street, Reading at 11.45pm. It was then that he was approached by an airman in uniform, who was missing his hat, collar and tie.

The airman identified himself as twenty-one-year-old Flight Sergeant Eric Pocock and said he was stationed at Lasham. He went on to say that he wished to give himself up as he had just strangled a woman inside a shop at number 54.

Pocock was taken into custody and Constable Haunton called in for assistance. Some thirty minutes after Pocock had handed

Friar Street, where the murder took place. Author's Collection

himself in, Constable Leslie Frederick Sawyer approached the confectioners and tobacconist's shop at 54 Friar Street to check out the report.

The front and rear doors were both locked, as were all the windows. At first it appeared that the report of a murder had been erroneous but then Sawyer shone his torch through the window, into the room behind the shop. There he could see something white in the shadows and, looking more closely, he saw that the shape appeared to be the naked legs of a woman.

A few minutes later, the police ambulance arrived, driven by Constable Hacker. The two officers then forced an entry through the front door and, going into the room at the rear, found the body of a woman lying on the floor. She was wearing only a slip and a bra. Other items of her clothing were in a tidy pile on a nearby table.

Doctor Michael Francis Murphy, the police surgeon, arrived on the premises at 12.23am on 2 September and officially pronounced life extinct. He noted that the woman lay on her back, with her feet pointing towards a fireplace and her head inclined towards the entrance doorway. Her hands were across her abdomen and her legs were extended and lightly apart. The doctor also noted that the deceased woman still had a sanitary towel in place.

Meanwhile, Detective Sergeant Leonard Robert Allen had arrived at Friar Street and he now made a careful search of the premises. An airforce cap, collar and tie were found in the room, along with a handbag which, presumably, belonged to the dead woman. Inside this, Sergeant Allen found a letter, which was addressed to Mrs Dobbs at *The Queens Arms*, 24 St Knollys Street, Reading. Opening the letter, Sergeant Allen began to read:

To my dear Mum and Dad,
By the time you receive this note I shall be gone from this world. Please don't grieve for me because this is what I want. I've lived my life and am happy to be going this way, and

please don't blame Mick. I am going of my own free will. This
way I leave Teddy free to marry again if he so desires, which is
more than he could do for me. All I asked was a devorce [sic]
which, after all, wasn't so much, if he loved me as much as he
said.
Goodbye and God bless you all. Connie.

The dead woman was soon identified as twenty-nine-year-old
Constance Lillian Boothby, who lived with her parents at the
public house at 24 St Knollys Street. She was the manageress of
the shop where her body was found, and a key-holder of the
premises.

Back at the police station, Pocock was also examined by a
doctor and a small stab wound was discovered just above the
apex of his heart. This had, apparently, been caused by a pair of
scissors, also found at the crime scene, and fitted in with
Pocock's claim that this had been a suicide pact. He had killed
Constance and then tried to kill himself, but his nerve had failed
and he had decided to hand himself over to the police instead.
Nevertheless, by his own admission, Pocock was responsible for
Constance's death and so was charged with murder.

The inquest on Constance Boothby opened on 6 September,
before the coroner, Mr John Lancelot Martin. Only two
witnesses were called. The first of these, Arthur Dobbs, the girl's
father, gave evidence of identification. He was followed into the
witness box by Dr Eric Gardner, who had conducted the post-
mortem, and told the court that the cause of death was manual
strangulation. The proceedings were then immediately
adjourned *sine die*.

Pocock's trial took place at Reading on 11 October 1946 and
one of the first witnesses was Edward Albert Boothby, the
estranged husband of the victim. He testified that his wife had
been born on 17 June 1917 and they had married on 4 August
1941. They had lived in Edgware and there were no children to
the union.

On 11 June 1945, Constance had left Edward and moved back to her parents' house. It was true that she had written to him, in September of that same year, to ask him for a divorce but they had not discussed the matter in detail and he had certainly never refused to grant her request.

Details of the first time Constance had met the man who would eventually take her life were given by Constance's sister, Edith May Dobbs. Edith also lived at the public house owned by her parents and she told the court that she and her sister often went to the Olympia Dance Hall situated on London Street, in Reading. It was there, about a month before she died, that Constance met an airman named Mick. That airman was, of course, Pocock, and Mick was his nickname.

On 1 September, the day that Constance died, Edith went to see her at the shop at around 5.20pm. Some twenty minutes later, Pocock arrived and the three of them talked as Constance cashed up. They all left the shop together, at 6.00pm and went to the Vaudeville Cinema on Broad Street. They didn't see a

Broad Street where Pocock went with Constance Boothby on the day he killed her. Author's Collection

Another view of Broad Street. Author's Collection

film, though, but had tea in the café there. Edith left them at 6.30pm and at that time they seemed happy enough in each other's company. Edith gave one last piece of information to the court: she did not recognise the writing on the letter as that of her sister.

Constance's parents, Arthur and Lilian Frizwide Elizabeth Dobbs, both gave statements that they did not recognise the writing on the letter as that of their daughter. Lilian, however, did point out that Constance had been ambidextrous and could write with either hand, though she usually used her left.

The disputed handwriting was also referred to by Lionel George Douglas Burnham, the owner of the shop where Constance had been found dead. He confirmed that she had worked for him since 9 October, 1945 but was unable to say that the writing was Constance's. Lionel's wife, Dorothy Ethel Burnham, was also unable to identify it.

Violet Trussler was a waitress in the café at the cinema and she confirmed that Constance, a woman she knew as the 'girl from the sweet shop', had come into the café on 1 September with another woman and an airman in uniform. She had later picked out Pocock at an identity parade.

Vera Grant was another waitress and she confirmed Violet's testimony, and said that Constance and the airman seemed to be quite friendly together. Vera too had picked out Pocock at the parade.

There were two other witnesses from that same café. Florence Gosnell, another waitress, had also seen Pocock and Constance together and had also made a positive identification at the parade. Finally, Marjorie Marshall was the cashier on the till. She too had seen an airman with Constance but failed to point out Pocock as that airman.

After leaving the café, Pocock and Constance had gone to the saloon bar at the *Jack of Both Sides* public house, arriving there at some time between 7.15pm and 7.30pm. This was confirmed by Jacynth Deirdrie Gardner, who had sat at a table with an airman and a young lady. Miss Gardner remembered that the airman had three stripes on his arm. He drank whisky whilst the girl he was with drank gin and orange. They left together at 10.00pm and were very friendly with each other.

Constable Haunton confirmed that he was in Friar Street, just passing the Harris Arcade, when Pocock approached him and said: 'I have just killed somebody. It was at 54 Friar Street, Reading and the person was a girl known as Connie Boothby.'

Constable Sawyer said that he had been at the Central police station when he received a call to take the ambulance to Friar Street where a body had been reported. Later, constable Hacker assisted him in forcing open the front door.

Pocock persisted in his claim that he and Constance had been involved in a suicide pact. They had had a pleasant night out together and after leaving the public house, had gone to the shop where they had sex together in the back room. Afterwards, they had discussed their predicament and since Constance was unable to get a divorce, it seemed that they just couldn't be together. They agreed that the only way out was to end their lives. He had then strangled her, after she had written the note to her parents, and then tried to stab himself to death, but failed. He was responsible for Constance's death but this was a case of manslaughter, not murder.

In the event, the jury did not agree and found Pocock guilty as charged, but they did add a recommendation to mercy. The law, however, allowed for only one possible sentence and Pocock was condemned to death. He was then moved to Oxford prison to await execution.

A subsequent appeal having failed, Pocock's death sentence was confirmed, but in fact he was to avoid the hangman's noose. On 23 October 1946, the sentence was commuted to one of life imprisonment and Pocock was removed from the condemned cell.

CHAPTER 10

A Blue Silk Scarf
George Russell
1948

Kathleen Cronin was a nurse at Maidenhead Hospital but by May 1948, she had decided on a slight change of career. Kathleen had come to the conclusion that she might well be happier working as a housekeeper or maid for an elderly lady or gentleman and, as a result, had registered with an agency. That agency had on their books an eighty-nine-year-old lady, who lived alone and was in need of a maid to attend to her needs. So it was that at around 9.00pm on Saturday 29 May 1948, Kathleen Cronin called at Wynford.

Wynford was a rambling and rather run down house, situated in its own grounds in Ray Park Avenue, Maidenhead. It was in this somewhat dilapidated twenty-two-room house that Minnie Freeman Lee lived alone and, by all accounts, this would not be an easy position for Miss Cronin for, apparently, Mrs Lee was a rather cantankerous old lady who treated people rather badly.

Kathleen Cronin knocked on the front door and rang the bell. Mrs Lee was known to be rather deaf and for that reason the doorbell was very loud. However, despite ringing many times, Kathleen did not receive a reply and there seemed to be no sign of life in the house. By the time Kathleen left, it was close to 9.30pm.

A few days later, at 9.30am on Tuesday 1 June, the local milkman was about to leave another pint at Wynford, when he noticed that there were three bottles still on the front doorstep. Two were completely full and the third was almost full, due to the fact that the foil top had been removed, presumably by birds, who had then consumed some of the contents. There was also a folded and apparently unread copy of the *Evening Standard*, dated 31 May.

Concerned that Mrs Lee might have been taken ill, the milkman walked into the badly overgrown back garden where he found Arthur Thomas Hilsdon, who worked in the grounds. Asked if he had seen the old lady recently, Hilsdon replied that he had not. He too then went to the front door and rang the bell a few times. When there was no reply, Hilsdon telephoned for the police.

It was 9.50am by the time Constable George Ernest Langton arrived at Wynford, with Mr Kenneth Ruffe Thomas, a magistrate's clerk and Mrs Lee's solicitor. The two men rang the bell and, receiving no reply, went around the back of the house. There they noticed that one of the windows, although closed and locked, was rather insecure so they forced it open and entered the house.

It was through these windows that Constable Langton gained entrance to the house.
The National Archives

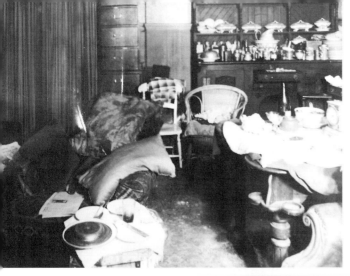

*One of the untidy rooms
inside the house.*
The National Archives

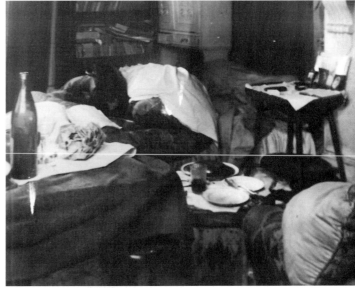

*Another view of the same
room showing the filthy state
the house was in.*
The National Archives

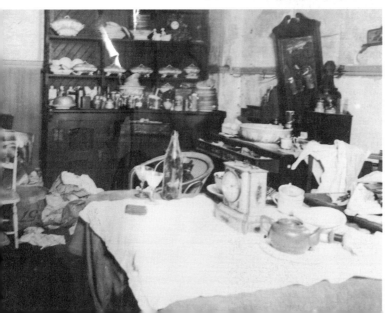

*Every room inside
Wynford was in this
same chaotic state.*
The National Archives

The back garden at Wynford, the house where Minnie Freeman Lee met her death. The National Archives

Every room was in a filthy state and had obviously not been cleaned or tidied for years. The two men passed from room to room, but there was no sign of Mrs Lee. Unsure what to do next, Constable Langton picked up the telephone, rang his station and reported what he had discovered to Superintendent Benstead. Even as the constable was on the telephone, Mr Thomas noticed a large leather trunk, fastened with straps.

Thinking that there might be a clue as to where Mrs Lee might have gone, Thomas unfastened the straps and lifted the lid of the trunk. Inside he saw what appeared to be nothing but a collection of old clothes but when he removed one or two of the topmost items he saw a woman's body beneath. Mrs Minnie Freeman Lee had been found.

The trunk in which Minnie's body was discovered.
The National Archives

Mrs Lee's arms were tied tightly behind her back and her legs had been bent at the knees so that she would fit inside the trunk. Her face and neck were covered with a towel which had been tied tightly around her. She was, quite obviously, dead and Constable Langton immediately informed the superintendent of this fact.

Superintendent Benstead and other officers were soon on the scene. Detective Sergeant Cyril Arthur Warren made a search of the premises and noted that, in addition to the milk bottles and newspaper on the front step, there was also an unopened letter behind the door. This was postmarked London SW1 and was dated 31 May 1948.

Warren also noted that Minnie's body was fully clothed, apart from her shoes, and her false teeth were still in her mouth. He took measurements of the trunk and recorded them as three feet nine inches, by two feet, by one foot six inches. Although all of

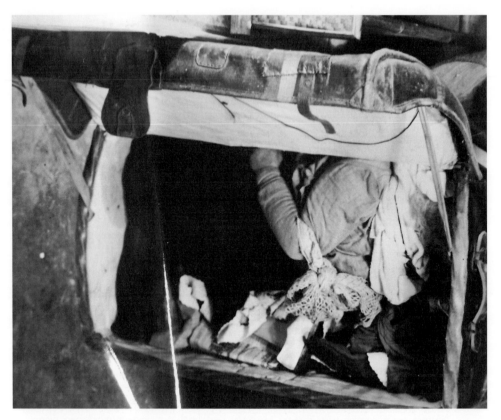

The trunk opened. Minnie's body can be seen inside. The National Archives

the rooms were in the same filthy state there were signs that drawers had been pulled out and ransacked. It appeared that this had been a robbery, which had ended in murder.

It was obviously important to determine, as precisely as possible, when Mrs Lee had been attacked. Various neighbours and local tradesmen were spoken to and this led officers to interview Edwin Stanley Tebbutt.

Mister Tebbutt ran an electrical goods shop from premises at 7 Guinions Road, High Wycombe, and he reported that Mrs Lee had called at his shop at 3.30pm on 29 May. She had told him that an electric boiling ring she had at home was broken and demanded that he come back with her, immediately, to repair it.

Mr Tebbutt pointed out that he was alone in the shop and couldn't simply close it up to attend to her request. Finally, after much argument, Mrs Lee purchased a new ring and allowed Mr Tebbutt the luxury of coming to fit it after he had closed the shop at the end of the business day.

At 6.20pm that same night, Mr Tebbutt had gone to Wynford. He told the police that upon going inside he found that the place stank so badly that he had to light a cigarette. He fitted the new ring and repaired a rather badly fitted electric plug whilst Mrs Lee chatted to him. At one point she said that she had bought some salmon for her dinner but complained about the six shillings she had had to pay. He left the house after some thirty minutes or so, pleased to be out in the fresh air again.

This was the last sighting of Mrs Lee alive and was a most important piece of evidence. It must be remembered that when Kathleen Cronin called at Wynford at 9.00pm that same evening, there was no reply to her constant ringing of the doorbell. At this stage, then police firmly believed that Minnie Freeman Lee had been attacked some time between 6.50pm and 9.00pm on Saturday 29 May.

Back at the house, an important clue was discovered. Amongst the items scattered about the floor was an old jewellery box. This was dusted for fingerprints and a partial print was discovered. This was soon identified as belonging to a habitual criminal named George Russell.

Russell was certainly well known to the police. He had twenty-one convictions, the first being dated 16 November 1927 and the last being 10 October 1947. He had been to prison twenty times for offences including stealing money, housebreaking, shopbreaking, larceny, malicious damage and an assault upon the police. His description was now widely circulated and forces throughout the country were told to be on the lookout for him.

Eventually, on 6 June, Russell was traced to the Ostler Hills Casual Hospital at St Albans. There, at 3.45am, he was arrested by Sergeant RA Porter who told him he would be taken to the

the following articles :-

3/6 in silver.
An Army discharge Book
An A.B. 64
A shaving brush and safety razor.
A table knife
2 combs
A handkerchief
A blue silk scarf
He was detined at St Albans Police

the arrival of an escort from Maidenhea

At no time during the remainder of

The police list of Russell's belongings. The words 'A blue silk scarf' have been added later. The National Archives

police station for interview. It was there that he was searched and a list of his belongings made. That list read: three shillings and six pence in silver coin, an Army discharge book, a shaving brush, a safety razor, a table knife, two combs, a handkerchief and a blue silk scarf. That last item would put George Russell on trial for his life.

Meanwhile, Russell made a full statement, detailing his movements. In this he claimed that he had spent a couple of days at the Henley Institution, a hostel, which he left on Friday 28 May. From there he had gone to Maidenhead, where did some gardening work for a woman who later complained about the five shillings he charged her. He then walked into the town where he met James Stock, who was working at Wynford. The two fell into conversation and that night Russell stayed with Stock and his wife in their lodgings.

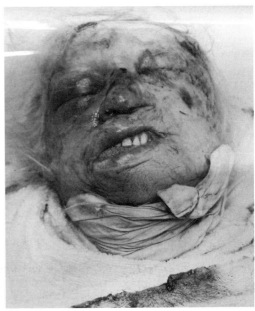

Minnie Freeman Lee in death, showing the linen tied tightly around her throat. The National Archives

Minnie Freeman Lee in her younger days. The National Archives

The next night, 29 May, he left Maidenhead at 7.30pm and walked to Old Windsor where he slept in a horse-shed, making up a bed from old coats. He rose at 5.30am on Sunday 30 May and walked to Staines, were he had a drink in a coffee shop opposite the police station.

From there he walked off towards London and earned a few shillings by doing some singing in the street just outside Staines. Then, on Monday 31 May, he went to Brighton where he slept at the Brighton Institution. The next day he went to Epsom, then on to Rowton House in Camden Town and finally on to St Albans, where he was arrested. He denied ever having set foot inside Mrs Lee's house, let alone being responsible for her death.

The statement was, of course, checked out. Officers spoke to Mr Cyril John Cook of College farm, Old Windsor. He confirmed that he owned a number of stables and at 6.00am on Saturday 30 May, he had gone into one of those stables to find that someone had made up a bed using some sacks and a couple of old coats.

This left the police with a major problem. If, as they suspected, and as all the medical evidence seemed to indicate, Mrs Lee had been attacked some time on the evening of 29 May, then Russell had an excellent alibi. He was at Old Windsor then and could not be responsible for her death. Nevertheless, Russell was charged with murder and sent for trial.

That trial opened at Reading on 13 October 1948, before Mr Justice Hallett. The proceedings lasted until 16 October, during which time the case for the Crown was led by Mr AJ Long, assisted by Mr JF Bourke. Russell was defended by Mr Eric Sachs and Mr GG Baker.

Two important pieces of evidence seemed to link George Russell to the death of Minnie Freeman Lee. The first of these was the fingerprint, found on the jewellery box, and the second was the blue silk scarf found in his possession when he was arrested at St Albans.

It wasn't really disputed that the box had belonged to Mrs Lee, but, nevertheless, the prosecution called Winifred Anne Wall, who had once worked for Mrs Lee. She testified that she had seen the box in Wynford many times and had often dusted it.

Of greater importance was the silk scarf. The prosecution called Christina Hayman, who was one of the few real friends that Mrs Lee had had. Christina testified that she had first met Minnie some thirty-six years before and since then they had often visited each other's homes. She admitted that Minnie could be rather careful with money and never paid any of her bills until it was absolutely necessary, usually when she received reminders or final demands. This had led to local gossip that she was a rich old woman with a great deal of cash hidden in the house.

Referring to the blue silk scarf, Christina said that it looked very much like one Minnie had owned, though she could not confirm that it was the exact one. As for Minnie's routine, Christina knew that she never went to bed early.

William Walter Bawden was a general dealer of 6 Harrow Close, Maidenhead and he had known Minnie for some twenty years. He had seen her with a blue silk scarf which she used to drape around her shoulders when she went out or sat in her back garden. He was almost positive that the scarf produced in court was the same one.

James Stock lodged at the *Gardeners Arms* public house at 45 Bridge Street, Maidenhead. He told the court that on Friday 28 May, he was rebuilding a wall at Wynford. This had been damaged in recent floods and he recalled that at one stage Mrs Lee had come out and told him, in no uncertain terms, that the name on the front gate needed repainting and he should see to it.

Some time just before 2.30pm, George Russell came up and began talking to him. Russell explained that he had just done some gardening for a woman in Maidenhead and Stock asked him if he might be interested in doing some work for the old woman who lived at Wynford. Russell had taken one look at the overgrown garden and said it was too big a job for him. He did pass on that the woman he had just worked for needed a cherry tree pruning and Stock might be interested in that.

The two men got on so well that they arranged to meet up later, in the *Gardeners Arms*. At 6.30pm, Russell did indeed come into the pub and had a conversation with Stock and the landlord, Mr Carter. Later, Stock and Russell were left alone and it was then that Russell asked him if he were interested in 'doing' the house where he was working.

Stock said he wasn't, mainly because the police would be on to him immediately as a suspect. To this, Russell said he knew a place where he could get some carpets, without doing any breaking and entering. When Stock asked where, Russell had said it was just down the road. The two men then went down Bridge Street and Russell told Stock to wait and keep watch whilst he went into a garage. He returned, moments later, with a rolled up carpet under his arm which they took back to the *Gardeners Arms*.

That night Stock and his wife, Florence, asked Russell to stay and he slept on a settee. Russell left the house very early the next morning but was back there by 8.00am. Later that same day, 29 May, Russell went back to Wynford where Stock was working again. It was just beginning to rain, so the two men went for a drink in the *Thames Hotel*, where they stayed until noon. That evening, Stock and Russell were back in the *Gardeners Arms* but, at around 7.00pm, Stock noticed that Russell had left without saying goodbye. He had not seen him again until now, at the trial.

Russell had said that he had bought the blue silk scarf from a man at a Salvation Army Hostel, and this transaction had been witnessed by a man named Alfred Radcliffe. That gentleman was now called to give his evidence. He confirmed that he had indeed been staying at the hostel in Great Peter Street, Westminster, up until around 4 June. A few days before that, he had met up with Russell and confirmed that he had purchased some underwear from another resident there. He could not, however, recall Russell buying a blue silk scarf.

On the final day of the trial, the jury retired to consider their verdict. After one hour and fifty minutes they returned to announce that Russell was guilty as charged. He made no comment as the death sentence was passed.

An appeal was heard, before the Lord Chief Justice, Lord Goddard and Justices Humphries and Lewis, on 15 November. Here it was claimed that the fingerprint found on the jewellery box was only a partial print and did not tie Russell to the crime, and that the trial judge had misdirected the jury in regard to the silk scarf. Both points were dismissed, the appeal was lost and Russell's fate was sealed.

On Thursday 2 December 1948, forty-five-year-old George Russell was hanged at Oxford prison. It was the seventh execution in a year that saw nine men hanged: two in Wales, one in Scotland and six in England. There remains, however, a number of unanswered questions.

In the first place, if George Russell had indeed broken into Wynford and robbed and killed Mrs Lee, why was it that the only thing he had apparently taken was a blue silk scarf? There is also the fact that if one looks at the original typed list of property found on Russell, one can see that the words 'A Blue Silk Scarf' have been added, presumably at a different time. Then we have the fact that when it seemed that Russell might have a cast-iron alibi for the originally perceived time of the murder, Dr Keith Simpson, the pathologist, adjusted his findings to say that Mrs Lee might have died at any time between 1.00am and 1.00pm on 30 May. In addition to this, it was clear that if Russell were the killer, he did not wear gloves since it was claimed that his print had been found on the jewellery box. Why was only one print ever found?

Finally, we have the curious statement, which Russell is supposed to have made to the police at St Albans when told that he was being investigated on a charge of murdering Mrs Lee. He is said to have replied: 'Did I murder this poor woman for something she was supposed to have, and had not?' The inference was that Russell had heard the local rumours of Mrs Lee having money hidden in the house, but hadn't found any.

It may well be that George Russell was guilty of the murder of Minnie Freeman Lee, but there is also the possibility that the evidence was adjusted to fit a suspect with a long criminal record.

CHAPTER 11

Fire!
Donald Zombie Batholomew Walton
1963

Nicholas Goodchild, a bus driver for the Reading Borough Council, was just starting his shift on the morning of 9 January 1963, when he spotted smoke coming from the building at 16-18 London Street.

The building at that location was Brennan's General Store but Goodchild knew that there were a number of flats on the upper floors of the building and people might possibly be trapped in there. He shouted to his conductor who ran to dial 999 from a nearby telephone box, whilst Goodchild ran to the building and tried to raise the alarm.

The fire brigade were on the scene within minutes but the premises were already a raging inferno. The store was mainly built of wood, and the fire had, by now, spread rapidly through the premises. Nevertheless, no fewer than seventeen people were rescued from the fire and only seven had to be taken to hospital for further treatment. Of those seven, only three had to be kept in hospital overnight: Annie Greenfield and Michael Crawley, who were both suffering from slight burns, and June Hardie who had fractured one of her heels in escaping. However, once the fire had been brought under control, officers found a single body in the bedroom of a flat on the third floor, that of eighty-two-year-old Georgina Taylor, who had lived in the building for some twenty-four years.

It soon became clear that the fire had almost certainly been started deliberately. Fire officers had determined that the seat of the fire had been a number of wooden and cardboard boxes, which had been left close to the stairwell on the ground floor. They had caught fire easily and soon spread to the stairwell itself, which then acted as a funnel, forcing the flames and smoke upwards and trapping the occupants. It was fortunate indeed that only one fatality had occurred.

The police, however, did not have to look too far in order to find the culprit. At 8.20am on the morning of the fire, a man walked into the police station and announced: 'I think I caused that fire, quite by accident mind you. It just shows what a single match can do. I lit half a fag and threw the match away. That must have started it.'

The man identified himself as Donald Walton and made a full written statement in which he said that he had first arrived in Reading on 11 December 1962, and lodged initially at the Salvation Army Hostel, also in London Street. Later, he had moved to new lodgings, at 55 Argyle Street. However, what Walton was claiming was a tragic accident, was believed to be something more for when officers checked up on Mr Walton they discovered that he had a long history of mental instability, had been in various institutions and, indeed, had escaped from one the previous year.

Despite his mental history, Walton was charged with manslaughter and, after various remands before the magistrates, was sent to face his trial at Oxford, which opened before Mr Justice Stable on 15 February.

The only witnesses called were medical gentleman as it was clear that Walton's mental condition meant that he would not be able to enter a plea to the charge.

Doctor Edmund Hemsted had performed the post-mortem on Georgina Taylor and confirmed that the cause of death was carbon monoxide poisoning, asphyxia and shock.

Doctor James Orr was the medical officer at Winchester prison where Walton had been held. He had observed the prisoner since his reception and had come to the conclusion that he was of unsound mind.

Doctor Bertram Mantelbroke was a consultant psychiatrist at the Littlemore Hospital and had made a number of examinations of the prisoner. Dr Mantelbroke testified that Walton had a history of sudden violent outbreaks and his moods fluctuated widely from day to day. He agreed that Walton was insane and unfit to plead.

Mister Justice Stable listened to the arguments on Walton's sanity and then addressed the jury saying: 'If a man was to be tried on a criminal charge he must have the mental facilities to follow all the proceedings, to instruct his lawyers, and to defend himself.' He then directed the jury to return a verdict that Walton was unfit to plead to the charge.

The jury obeyed that direction, Walton was then ordered to be detained during Her Majesty's pleasure. It was, perhaps, little consolation for the family and friends of Georgina Taylor.

CHAPTER 12

Fingerprints
Benjamin Frank Achilles Comas
1966

On 31 March 1966, seventy-one-year-old Alice Beatrice Cox spent a pleasant afternoon shopping in Reading. Beatrice was with her married daughter who saw her to her bus stop, where the two women parted at approximately 6.15pm.

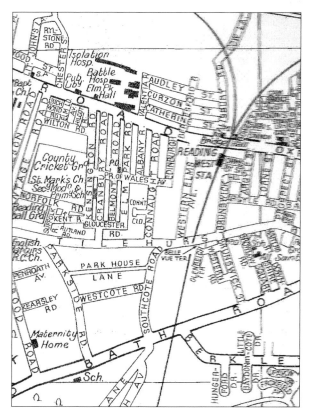

The area around Reading West station, showing where the murder took place. Author's Collection

Not long after this, at some time between 6.30pm and 6.45pm, Cecily Elaine Wood, Mrs Cox's next door neighbour, saw Alice in the garden of her home at 55 Salisbury Road, Reading. For the rest of the evening, all was quiet in Salisbury Road.

At 1.00am the following morning, 1 April, Mrs Avenell, who lived at number 59, was woken by the sound of a window rattling nearby and what sounded like a woman screaming. As she strained to hear for any other sounds, Mrs Avenell heard nothing more and drifted off back to sleep.

At 10.15am that same morning, Mrs Sear, who lived next door to Alice Cox at number 53, spoke to Elsie Edith Porton who lived on the other side of the road, almost directly opposite. The two ladies were growing rather concerned. Mrs Cox was a creature of habit and was usually up and about by this time of day. The curtains were still drawn at number 55 and there was no activity to be seen.

Elsie Porton had a key to number 55, given to her by Alice Cox in case of emergencies. Perhaps the old lady had been taken ill and it would surely be nothing more than neighbourly to check on her. Elsie took her key and gingerly unlocked the front door of Alice Cox's house but immediately she could see that something must be wrong. The house, normally neat and tidy, was in a state of disarray. Not sure what she should do next, Elsie returned to her own home and telephoned for Mrs Cox's son.

Harry Arthur Cox soon arrived and he now went into his mother's house, accompanied by Mrs Sear and Mrs Porton. The house was indeed in disarray and, as they passed from room to room, it became clear that someone had broken in and ransacked the place. Going upstairs, Harry Cox found his mother lying in bed with one of her legs dangling over the side. She appeared to be dead and Harry dashed back downstairs and telephoned for the police.

Constable Edward White was the first officer to arrive. He

noted that the bedroom curtains were still drawn, a point that would prove to be crucial later, and then removed a bolster from the bed in order to confirm that Alice Cox was indeed dead. Then, mindful of a need to preserve the crime scene, Constable White replaced the bolster and waited for other officers to arrive.

The police soon determined that the most likely scenario was that this was a robbery, which had gone wrong. Someone had broken into the house by smashing a window at the rear and since only a sixpence and a half-penny had been found in the house, it was reasonable to assume that other cash had been stolen. Perhaps Mrs Cox had disturbed the burglar, or woken when he smashed the window or came into her room. Either way, she had then been subdued, stabbed, although that wound was only slight, and subsequently suffocated.

No time was wasted in seeking the help of Scotland Yard. The same day that the body was discovered, a telegram was sent to London, asking for assistance. So it was that Detective Superintendent Herbert Guiver and Detective Sergeant Leslie Emment travelled over to Reading to take charge of the case.

A very large number of fingerprints were found inside the house at 55 Salisbury Road. Meticulously a list was drawn up of anyone with legitimate access to the house such as friends, relatives, neighbours and even tradesmen. Their fingerprints were taken for elimination purposes and after all that had been done, one set of prints remained unidentified. These almost certainly belonged to the intruder but the problem was that, whoever that person was, he had no criminal record. His prints were not on file with the police.

It was then that Superintendent Guiver decided that the only way forward was a mass fingerprinting of all males within the area. Over the next few days, officers called at homes and workplaces and took more than 10,000 sets of prints. None of them matched the set found at Salisbury Road.

It was 23 April, more than three weeks after Alice's body had been found, when Constable Allan Charles Kennerley called at 3 Cambridge Place to take the fingerprints of a lodger there, a man who went by the name of Frank. Going into Frank's room, Kennerley saw that it was in a state of disorder but of Frank, there was no sign. The officer decided that he would have to call back at another time.

In fact, Kennerley returned later that same day, accompanied by Detective Sergeant Ivor Dyer but there was still no sign of Frank. Determined not to miss out on fingerprinting a possible suspect, the two officers decided that they should fingerprint certain items within the room, including a tin of boot polish, which had an excellent surface for holding prints. After all, they reasoned, the occupant must have touched the items and it was just as valid a way of obtaining his prints. In fact, it was a very wise decision indeed for when the prints of the elusive Frank were checked, they were found to be a match to those left at the crime scene.

Further checking revealed that Frank was actually Benjamin Frank Achilles Comas, a native of St Vincent in the Caribbean. A full description was circulated and all officers were warned to be on the lookout for him. In fact, the very next day, 24 April, Constable Kennerley and Constable Hounslow were in the centre of Reading when they spotted a man fitting Comas' description sitting in a café.

The two officers went in to speak to the man and asked for his name and address. He said that he was Benjamin Brown and lived at 11 Waylen Street. Not satisfied with his explanation, the suspect was taken to the police station and asked to give his fingerprints for comparison. Brown refused at first, claiming that he had already given them as part of the mass fingerprinting of the area. Told that he would be detained, Brown finally agreed to give his prints. They were duly checked and found to be a match for those found at both Salisbury Road and Cambridge Place. Benjamin Brown was none other than Benjamin Comas and he was then duly charged with murder, wounding with intent, housebreaking with intent to steal, and larceny.

After various appearances before the magistrates, Comas faced his trial on the four charges on 11 July 1966, before Mister Justice Stable. The trial lasted until 14 July, during which Comas was defended by Mr Douglas Draycott and Mr RM Talbot. The case for the prosecution was led by Mr F Blennerhassett assisted by Mr John Wood. Asked how he wished to plead, Comas replied that he wished to plead guilty to housebreaking, but was then spoken to by his defence barrister. After some discussion, Comas changed his plea to not guilty on that charge and the charge of murder, but did plead guilty to housebreaking with intent. He was basically admitting that he had broken into Alice Cox's house but had not taken anything and was not responsible for her death.

A total of twenty-nine witnesses appeared for the prosecution, many of them serving police officers. However, another one of the most important witnesses was a gentleman named Mark Fletcher.

Mark Fletcher lived next door to Alice Cox, at 57 Salisbury Road. He testified that three years before Alice's death, Comas had called at his house, asking for lodgings. Mr Fletcher owned a couple of houses in the area and was known to take in lodgers. He agreed to take in Comas, who then stayed with him for about a year before moving on. Some six weeks before Alice's death, Comas had returned to Fletcher's house and asked for lodgings again. This time he was given a room in another of Fletcher's properties, at 3 Cambridge Place. Comas moved into that address on 27 March 1966 and Fletcher had not seen his tenant since that date.

This testimony was important because it contradicted what Comas had told the police after his arrest. Comas had begun by denying any involvement whatsoever in the break in at 55 Salisbury Road. Faced with the fingerprint evidence he then changed his story and claimed that he had broken in but it was paid by Fletcher to do it.

Comas claimed that he had borrowed £30 from Fletcher but

was unable to repay it. Fletcher had suggested that he would pay him to break into the old lady's house next door. No sooner had this claim been made than Comas changed his story slightly, saying that he had only broken in so that he could get some money to repay the loan to Fletcher, again at the latter's instigation.

A third statement was then made in which Comas now claimed that he had not been alone in the house. Fletcher had now been with him and if anyone was responsible for killing Alice Cox, then it was Fletcher. Finally, a fourth version had it that Comas had broken in alone and Fletcher had not been present after all.

Every part of these various statements was totally denied by Mark Fletcher. He said that he had not seen Comas for six weeks and had never been in Alice Cox's house. This was confirmed, in part, by Cecily Elaine Wood, who lodged with Fletcher at number 57. She agreed that Comas had not been back to the house after his visit in March.

The judge summed up the case on the fourth day of the trial. The jury retired at 2.20pm and returned to court at 3.55pm to announce that they had found Comas guilty of all the charges. As a result, Comas was sentenced to life imprisonment for murder and also received sentences of fifteen years for wounding with intent and fourteen years for housebreaking and larceny.

An appeal was entered but dismissed on 17 January 1967. Comas, however, was not prepared to let the matter rest there. On 7 July 1967, he wrote a long letter to Superintendent Guiver, from Wormwood Scrubs prison, seeking that Mark Fletcher should be charged with perjury.

The letter was littered with errors of grammar and spelling, but in it Comas claimed to have proof that Mark Fletcher had lied in court. Comas claimed to have a finance form for the purchase of a car, countersigned by Fletcher acting as guarantor and dated 1962. In his evidence, Fletcher had said that he first met Comas three years before the crime, that is, in 1963.

The letter, written by Comas from Wormwood Scrubs prison, after his conviction. The National Archives

In addition, Fletcher had said that he had never seen Comas again after March 1966, but Comas now claimed to have proof that Fletcher had written a letter for him, to the Social Security office, on 6 April. Finally, Comas stated that if he did not receive satisfaction, he would take his case to the European Commissioner in Strasbourg.

The police were satisfied that there was no grain of truth in this and no action was taken against Mark Fletcher. Comas had lied repeatedly after his arrest and changed his story four times. The authorities believed that he had acted alone and was solely responsible for the death of Alice Cox, and a jury had agreed with that premise.

CHAPTER 13

The Red Mini Murder
Raymond Sidney Cook, Eric Jones and Valerie Dorothy Newell
1967

At approximately 9.55pm on Thursday 2 March 1967, Robin Anthony Franklin and Colin Pinfield were driving up Cock's Hill in Rumerhedge Wood in Peppard, Oxfordshire, when they passed a dark-coloured Cortina parked on a bend in the road. The car had its boot open, and the headlights were off, though the sidelights were still on. There was no sign of any occupant.

The two men continued on their journey and some one hundred yards further on they saw a red Mini, half on and half off the road. There was a woman lying on the ground close to the driver's door and a man was bending over her, presumably trying to give what assistance he could. There was a third man at the scene, sitting in the front passenger seat and he appeared to be trying to get out of the car.

Robin stopped his car and asked what he might do to help, having first sent Colin off to find a call-box and get an ambulance to come. As Robin took in the scene, the man who had been leaning over the stricken woman said that he had not

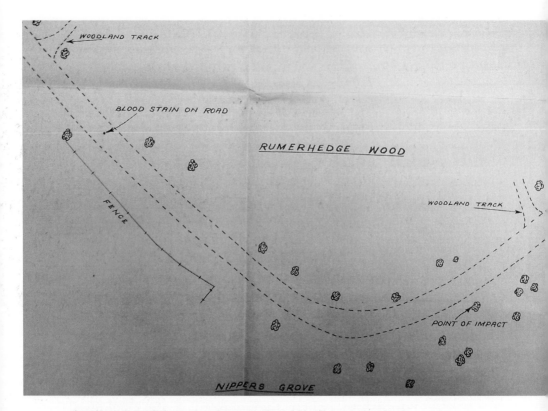

A police map of the area where the Red Mini Murder took place. The National Archives

been involved in the accident but had simply found the car, just as Robin had done. He then said he would go back to his own car and get some blankets. To Robin Franklin's surprise, the man never returned. Presumably he had climbed back into the Cortina up the road, and driven off.

Meanwhile, Colin Pinfield had arrived at Kate's Cottage, Witfold, where he roused Douglas Charles Edward Johns. Once Colin had explained that he and his friend had come across an accident up the road, and that they needed assistance, Johns dialled 999 and asked for an ambulance to be sent. As he then followed Colin back to the scene, his wife made a second telephone call, this time to the police.

That telephone call to the police caused Constable Stephen Sherlock to be directed to the scene of the accident and he arrived there at 10.50pm. The constable then noted a red Mini, registration 4499 DP, which had apparently left the road and collided with a beech tree. The officer also noticed that there was a substantial amount of blood inside the car, mainly on the driver's side and that the windscreen of the vehicle was intact. He also noted that, curiously, the ignition and headlights of the crashed vehicle were off, and the handbrake was on.

By this time, both of the occupants had been taken, by ambulance, to the Battle Hospital in Reading. Sherlock then spoke to the three men still at the scene, Mr Franklin, Pinfield and Johns, and obtained some initial details of what they had found. Constable Sherlock was also told of the mysterious man who had been with the female driver when Franklin and Pinfield had arrived, but who had then simply driven off.

The next thing to do was move the car. There seemed to be very little damage to the Mini. The front bumper was off, the off-side front wing was furled back onto the tyre and one headlight was smashed but Sherlock was able to bend the wing back a little and reverse the car back onto the road. He then asked Mr Johns to drive the Mini back to his garage.

Seeing that there was little more he could do at the scene, Constable Sherlock went back to his home at Nettlebed, taking with him, as evidence, a handbag he had found at the scene and which, presumably, had belonged to the female occupant of the vehicle. Then, just after midnight, he telephoned the Battle Hospital to inquire after the two injured occupants. He was surprised to be told that the male passenger seemed to be uninjured but the female driver had died from her injuries. Pausing only to report the matter to his headquarters, Sherlock then drove to the hospital to view the body of the dead woman.

Whilst he was at the hospital, Sherlock also took the opportunity to speak to the male passenger who identified himself as thirty-two-year-old Raymond Sidney Cook and said he was a draughtsman, living at 3 Farley View, Spencer's Wood, Reading. He also confirmed that the driver of the vehicle had been his wife, June Serina Cook, a forty-one-year-old schoolteacher, though he appeared to have little recollection of the accident itself.

The hospital had thought that Raymond Cook was drunk. His speech was slurred and he seemed somewhat dazed and incoherent. Constable Sherlock thought that this might be the after-effects of shock, due to the accident and, since he didn't appear to need any medical attention, offered to drive Cook home. On the way, the constable couldn't help but notice that the directions which Cook gave to his home were precise and clear. This seemed peculiar considering that, at the hospital, Cook had displayed signs of confusion. It was, perhaps, at this time that Constable Sherlock first began to have some suspicions about the accident.

Arriving at Cook's home, Sherlock called out the family doctor and arranged for a nurse to relieve the babysitter who had been taking care of Cook's two children. Whilst waiting for these people to arrive, Sherlock discovered that the dead woman's parents actually lived next door, so took the opportunity to rouse them and give them the tragic news that their daughter had died in a car accident. Here, Constable Sherlock's suspicions were added to when it became clear that June Cook's parents did not approve of their son-in-law.

Sherlock had still not finished for the night. He drove to the police headquarters at Henley, and reported that he did not believe that the facts of the case were clear and he had his suspicions that the story he had been told did not explain June Cook's injuries, especially since her husband did not seem to be injured at all. He then drove back to the scene of the crash to make another examination. Finally, he sent another message to his headquarters, asking that a scenes of crime officer be sent out once it was light enough to see.

At 6.30am on Friday 3 March, Constable Sherlock was back at the garage where the crashed car had been taken. In the light he could see that there were blood spatters on the outside of the vehicle and what appeared to be a human hair, itself spattered with blood, was adhering to the paintwork over the rear wheel arch. Later still, Sherlock took a statement from Robin Franklin who had driven up to the scene of the crash. He then went back to Spencer's Wood to see Raymond Cook again.

A written statement was taken from Cook, who explained that he and his wife had been out together the previous night for a meal. They had gone to the *George Hotel* at Pangbourne and when they left, Cook himself was driving. After travelling a mile or so he felt sick and asked his wife if she wouldn't mind driving instead. She agreed and they changed places and he began to doze as they drove on. Suddenly he heard his wife call out. They were on a bend and a car was coming towards them with its headlights dazzling them both. He felt a bump and that was all he remembered until some men were trying to help him.

There was still the unexplained mystery of the first man at the scene, the driver of the dark-coloured Cortina, who had simply driven off. He might have been a witness to the accident itself or, indeed, been involved. It was essential that he be traced, so a message was sent to all police stations in the area to try to trace the driver of the Cortina.

Fortunately for the police, one of the first men at the scene was a fireman and therefore perhaps more observant than the average witness. He stated that the Cortina was not only dark in colour, but was actually dark blue. Further, it had a deluxe model grill and no wing mirrors. That made the vehicle more distinctive and therefore, hopefully, easier to trace.

On 4 March, Sherlock was back at the crash site with Detective Sergeant McMiken, the scenes of crime officer. He took a number of photographs of the damage to the beech tree, and the immediate area of the crash and then decided that he should take a long-shot of the bend where car went off the road. As McMiken set up his tripod some seventy-five yards from the crash site, he spotted a stain in the road, which appeared to be blood. This was pointed out to Constable Sherlock, who took a scrapping off the gravel before both men went to the garage to take further pictures, of the Mini.

The damaged car was then taken to Henley police headquarters where Sherlock reported his suspicions about the accident to Detective Inspector Issell. Meanwhile, the initial pathology report had been made on June Cook, and the best theory was that the only way Mrs Cook could have sustained the injuries she did was for her to have been thrown through the windscreen and then struck her head on the tree. Sherlock recalled, of course, that the windscreen of the Mini was intact. A second post-mortem was ordered.

By now, the whole affair was being treated as a suspicious death. Detective Issell and Constable Sherlock called on Raymond Cook again and asked to see the clothes he had been wearing on the night of the accident. Cook reported that he had sent them to the dry cleaners the day after the accident, that he had asked his mother to wash his shirt, and that he had burned the leather gloves he was wearing as they were bloodstained and therefore ruined.

The next port of call was June's parents next door. They now explained that they were not on good terms with Raymond because of the way he had treated their daughter. He had deserted her in the autumn of 1966 and gone to live with a woman who worked as a nurse at the Borocourt Mental Hospital. They were rather unsure of the woman's name but believed it might have been Kim Mule.

Police checks revealed that the woman Raymond Cook had had an affair with was Valerie Dorothy Newell, who preferred to use the first name Kim. She lived at 5 Sidmouth Street, Reading and apparently Cook had lived with her for some two months at the end of 1966, but had then returned to his wife. Two other interesting facts were also discovered.

The first of these was that June Cook was quite a wealthy woman. Her parents had given her the house next door to theirs as a wedding present, when she married Cook. She was also insured for £1000 in the event of death in a car accident. Further, she controlled the purse strings in the family. When Cook had left June, she had closed their joint bank account and cut him out of her will. When he returned to her, however, she had re-opened the bank account and again made him the main beneficiary under her will.

The second fact was that the affair between Raymond Cook and Kim Newell had not apparently ended. There was evidence that they continued to see each other on a very regular basis and Kim Newell was now pregnant. Was this, plus the money he would receive, a motive for Raymond Cook to murder his wife?

June Cook's funeral was scheduled to take place on 9 March but the police informed Cook that it would have to be postponed pending further enquiries. In addition, the inquest was also temporarily postponed. That same day, a request for assistance was telegraphed to the murder squad at Scotland Yard and two officers, Detective Superintendent Ian Forbes and Detective Sergeant Peter Hill, travelled from the capital to Reading.

One of the first steps for Superintendent Forbes was to have the red Mini taken to the forensic science laboratory in Holborn, where a thorough examination could be made. At about the same time, a most valuable witness came forward.

By now, details of the dark-blue Cortina, and the man who had driven off from the scene of the crash, had been circulated in the newspapers so that the public could offer their assistance. One of those press reports was seen by a house-painter named Angus Macdonald.

He told the police that he had seen a dark-blue Cortina,

with no wing-mirrors, being driven into Reading from the direction of Oxford. The car was being driven by a man but there was a woman passenger in the front seat, apparently giving him directions. By a remarkable coincidence, Macdonald was on his way to visit his mother, who lived next door to Kim Newell. Macdonald was, therefore, able to say that the woman passenger had been none other than Miss Newell. Further, Macdonald recalled the licence plate of the Cortina: 7711 FM.

The car was immediately traced, to a plant-hire company in Wrexham. Officers were despatched to the company on 12 March, and arrived just in time to see a man climbing into the car. He identified himself as forty-five-year-old Eric Jones of 176 Chester Road, Wrexham, and he said that on the day of the accident he had been in London. He had been to South Africa House in Trafalgar Square, but it was closed so later he had visited the Highgate area. He had certainly not been anywhere near Reading. For the time being at least, Jones was allowed to go.

In due course, the report on the red Mini came through from Holborn. All the blood on the vehicle was of the same type as June Cook's. It was heaviest on the driver's side of the car but there were blood spatters throughout the vehicle and also on the outside. Further, blood had been found on the passenger seat and this had seeped through into the fabric showing that there must have been no-one sitting in that seat when Mrs Cook began to shed blood. There was one final fact. The impact of the car into the beech tree had displaced some of the bodywork and bloodstains had been found in a position which meant that the impact must have taken place after the blood was shed.

At the same time, Dr Derek Barrowcliff had conducted a new post-mortem which showed that June Cook had suffered at least seven blows on the front of her head. In his opinion these had most probably been inflicted from above whilst she was in a kneeling position. This was not a tragic accident but a case of murder.

On 17 March, the inquest finally opened but after evidence of identification was given, the proceedings were immediately adjourned. That same day, Raymond Cook was arrested and charged with the murder of his wife.

On 22 March, Eric Jones was interviewed again, in Wrexham. After some intense questioning he admitted that he had once had a long affair with Kim Newell. Some six years ago she had even become pregnant by him but had an abortion. Jones now agreed that he had been in Reading on 2 March and had seen Newell to discuss the possibility of another abortion, but had told her that he was unable to help. Jones still denied any involvement in Mrs Cook's death.

The next day, 23 March, Kim Newell was taken to the police station at Reading, for interview. She confirmed that there had been a relationship with Eric Jones some six or seven years before and that Jones had called on her on the evening of 2 March. He didn't know the best route out of Reading so she went with him part of the way to direct him. She was back home by 7.40pm and had no involvement in the death of June Cook.

In fact, it wasn't until April that the case was finally broken. Kenneth Adams was the husband of Kim Newell's sister, Janet. He told the police that his wife had said that Kim had confided in her. Apparently, Kim had told Janet that Jones had killed June by striking her with a car jack. This was part of a conspiracy to kill June and, in fact, other arrangements had been made previously.

There had been some discussion about driving the car into the river near Woodley airfield but this had been called off. Even the present plan had been postponed until after June altered her will back to make her husband the beneficiary once again. Once this was done, June's fate was sealed. The plan was that Raymond would take his wife out for a meal. On the way home, Jones would flag their car down and pretend his own vehicle was having mechanical trouble. Then June would be battered to death and an accident faked. As to why Kim was telling Janet all this, Kenneth Adams explained that she was afraid that Jones might kill her in order to hide his own involvement and she wanted someone to know this, so that he could be arrested and charged.

On 16 April, Kim Newell was arrested and the following day, after being interviewed yet again, Eric Jones was taken into custody. He made a full written statement admitting his part in the affair and later, whilst being held in the cells, he made a full verbal statement to Constable Neville Jones Hughes who had been detailed to watch over the cells at Wrexham. Constable Hughes had only been out of training college for three weeks and may not have been fully conversant with the correct procedure, but he did note down in his pocketbook all that Jones said.

Jones was then transferred to Reading and the next day, 18 April, he and Newell were both charged with murder.

The trial of all three defendants opened at Oxford on 5 June 1967 before Mr Justice Stable. The case for the prosecution was led by Mr Brian Gibbins who was assisted by Mr JED Irving. Cook was defended by Mr Douglas Draycott and Mr Michael Talbot. Jones was represented by Mr Kenneth Jones and Mr Nigel Fricker, whilst Newell was defended by Mr William Howard and Mr Patrick Medd.

Originally, all three were charged with murder but in the early stages of the trial, the charge against Newell was reduced to being an accessory before the fact.

The third day of the proceedings were largely taken up with legal arguments, held in camera, during which Jones' defence team tried to exclude the confession he had made to officers at Wrexham. Jones was now claiming that this had been made under duress. The publicity these arguments generated in the newspapers was seen by Constable Hughes at Wrexham, who only now brought the notes he had made to the attention of his superiors. Since those notes, which were certainly not made under duress, were an almost exact copy of what Jones had said in his written confession, Hughes was called to Oxford to give evidence. Faced with this, on the fourth day of the trial, Jones changed his plea to guilty and then gave evidence for the Crown against the other two.

The proceedings lasted for twelve days and when the jury returned to court after a deliberation of some two hours, on 21 June, it was to announce that all three were guilty as charged. They all received sentences of life imprisonment.

It can perhaps be argued that the person at the centre of this web of deceit and intrigue had been Valerie Newell. She ended up serving twelve years in prison, being released in 1979. She moved to Wales and obtained a position as a schoolteacher. Some eleven years later, in 1990, she died of cancer. Perhaps she can best be summed up by her own words. Asked to speak about the crime, she said: 'Yes, I feel remorse. She didn't deserve to die.' Then, referring to the two men who had taken part with her in the crime she added: 'I never loved them. I only loved my dog.'

CHAPTER 14

The Gravel Pit Murders
David Burgess
1967

Jacqueline Williams and Jeanette Wigmore were the best of friends. The two nine-year-old girls were always together and things were no different on the evening of Monday 17 April 1967.

At some time between 4.30pm and 5.00pm on that Monday, the two girls left the village of Beenham on their bicycles, for a ride in the countryside. Shortly afterwards, at around 5.15pm, they were seen together by Jeanette's father, Anthony Wigmore, in Webbs Lane. Soon after that, at approximately 5.30pm, the two friends were seen by William Goody. By now the girls had dismounted from their bicycles and were pushing them along, close to the junction of Webbs lane and Admoor Lane.

Charles Gillings was working in that area from about 6.00pm onwards. At 6.25pm, having finished what he needed to do, Mr Gillings let his dog loose for a run in the fields around one of the gravel pits. As the animal scampered off, Mr Gillings noticed two children's bicycles lying on the grass near the entrance to the pit. Strangely, he could hear no sounds of laughter or children playing and saw no trace of whoever might own those bicycles.

By 7.30pm that same evening, Anthony Wigmore was growing concerned. It was not like Jeanette to stay out this late. He knew that when he had seen his daughter, she had been with her good friend Jacqueline, so his first port of call was the Williams' house. There he spoke to Jacqueline's father, Terence, and when he said that Jacqueline hadn't come home either, the two men set off, with others, to find their daughters.

Although the talk amongst the men looking for the two girls was of children staying out later than they should, the events of the previous year must have been at the back of everyone's minds. In October 1966, a seventeen-year-old nursemaid, Yolande Waddington, had been sexually assaulted, and murdered, in the village and the killer had never been found. Pushing such thoughts to the backs of their minds, the search party went on looking for the two girls.

It was then that Anthony Wigmore remembered that Jeanette had said something about getting some frog spawn for a nature study class at school. All the children in the area knew that the best place to get spawn was in the pools around the gravel pits and, of course, Anthony had seen Jeanette earlier, heading off in that direction with Jacqueline. Anthony decided that he would go up to the pits and bring the girls home, possibly with a flea in their ears for staying out so late.

Anthony drove up towards the pits and, entering the same field where Charles Gillings had been an hour or so before, he the same two bicycles, one of which he instantly recognised as Jeanette's. Walking on a little further, Anthony found his own daughter's body, lying in a shallow pool of water. She had, apparently, been killed by a single stab wound.

The police were called in and a search of the immediate area organised. Just before 11.00pm, Inspector Mutch of the Reading Police found the body of Jacqueline Williams. She lay some 120 yards from her friend, and had been drowned in six inches of water. There were also signs that she had been sexually assaulted. The police were looking for a double child-killer.

Determined that this should not be another unsolved murder in the village, the local police immediately sought the assistance of Scotland Yard. They responded by sending Detective Superintendent William Marchant to take charge of the investigation.

One of the first things Superintendent Marchant did was to organise a series of house-to-house checks. He had come to believe that since the gravel pits in the area were secluded, the killer was most probably a local man. Thus, all males were interviewed and asked to say where they had been between 5.30pm and 9.00pm, on the evening of Monday 17 April.

The villagers of Beenham offered every assistance to the investigating officers. People came forward to report sightings of strangers they had seen in and around the area. Thus, within days, police were trying to trace a cyclist, who had been seen in the village a few hours before the two girls had been murdered. He was described as being forty to forty-five years old, about five feet six inches tall, thick set and with grey or white hair. He had a full, ruddy face and was dressed in a checked shirt and a pinkish-brown windcheater or anorak. He had been seen parking his bicycle in a gateway, close to *The Stocks* public house.

Another sighting had been made of a woman, who had been using binoculars close to the Mayridge gravel pit. She was not a suspect but might well have seen something. She was soon traced but was unable to take the investigation any further.

Officers were also seeking to trace the driver of a Ford Zephyr car, which had been parked not far from the scene of the crime. That driver, too, was soon traced and eliminated from the inquiry.

The area around Beenham was soon crowded with newspaper reporters. Not only was this a double murder but now three females had been killed in the area within six months. One of those reporters, George Hollingbery, whilst looking around the village, found a bundle of soiled clothing, apparently dumped underneath a hedge. These items, a blue jacket and grey trousers, were handed into the police and subjected to forensic examination. No trace of blood, or any other evidence, was discovered.

The inquest on the dead girls opened before Mr Charles Hoile, at Newbury, on Friday 28 April. Only basic evidence of identification and the injuries the girls had received were given before the proceedings were adjourned.

By 5 May, over 4000 questionnaires had been completed by the police. Blood samples and statements had been taken from all the men aged between nineteen and sixty, who lived in and around Beenham. It was this painstaking approach which led Superintendent Marchant to narrow his search down to just one man.

David Burgess fitted the profile of the killer very well indeed. He was nineteen years old, a local man, and worked as a dumper-truck driver in Fisher's Pit, one of the gravel pits in Admoor Lane, close to where the girls had been found. On the day of the murder he had left work at 5.30pm and had been seen by other villagers in the area. Burgess worked with his brother, John, whom he told he was off to find some rabbit snares. He apparently returned to work soon afterwards, and was seen, by his brother, reading a book, at around 6.25pm.

There was one other curious piece of information. John Burgess had told the police that the day after the murders, Tuesday 18 April, he had casually mentioned to David that he had been missing from work at about the time the girls were killed and so might have had the opportunity to commit the crime. Instead of simply denying any involvement, David had snapped back: 'It wasn't me.'

David Burgess was taken in for questioning and his clothing taken for forensic examination. That examination revealed spots of blood on the side of one of Burgess' shoes and when that was tested it was found to be of the rare group ABMN. This was the same group as Jeanette's and only 1.5% of the population had such a group. It linked Burgess directly to Jeanette's body and he was now asked to explain it.

Burgess began by denying everything. He could offer no explanation as to how Jeanette's blood could have come to be on his shoe. Superintendent Marchant asked him again and again to account for this fact, but Burgess would only say he hadn't been in that particular gravel pit on that day. Finally, after what seemed an age, Burgess finally broke down in tears and shouted: 'You catch the man I chased away.'

Asked to elaborate, Burgess went on to say: 'I was up the end of my pit, where I work, when I heard someone scream. When I went across, I saw him. The bloke stood there and she was in the water. I shouted at him.'

Continuing his narrative, Burgess claimed that he had then gone to where Jeanette's body lay, and picked her up. He saw the blood on her and was sure that she was dead and there was nothing he could do for her. Rather than run for help, though, he simply placed her body back where he had found it and told no-one. He ended by claiming that he had never seen the body of Jacqueline.

The police believed that they had captured their killer and, on the evening of Sunday 7 May, Burgess was charged with the murder of Jeanette Wigmore. He made his first appearance before the magistrates on Monday 8 May, when matters were adjourned until Friday 12 May. Other adjournments followed and, on Friday 26 May, Burgess was also charged with the murder of Jacqueline Williams.

Burgess faced the magistrates for the last time in June 1967, when he was sent for trial at Gloucester. However, before that trial opened, Burgess had more information to give to the police.

The week before his trial was due to take place, Burgess said he wished to say more about the man he claimed to have seen with Jeanette's body. Now he recalled that the man was named Mac. He couldn't remember the exact surname but believed it might have been MacNab. Burgess claimed that he had first seen the man in the Viking Café on Caversham Road, Reading. He knew that Mac went there quite a lot so the police should have no trouble in tracing him.

Burgess went on to say that he had seen Mac again, after the murders, in the *Six Bells* public house at Beenham. Mac had followed Burgess to the toilets and warned him to keep his mouth shut about seeing him with the girl's body. The story was checked out and proved to be valueless. There was no regular customer at the Viking Café named Mac and no-one had seen such a man in the *Six Bells*.

David Burgess faced his trial for murder on Thursday 13 July 1967, before Mr Justice Stable and a jury of nine men and three women. The case for the prosecution was led by Mr Kenneth Jones, and Burgess was defended by Mr Douglas Draycott. The proceedings would last until 21 July.

Burgess was questioned closely about his not reporting finding the body of Jeanette Wigmore, if his story was true. He claimed that he had not reported it as he did not wish to become involved. It did not, apparently, matter that had he raised the alarm, the killer might have been captured immediately. Nor did it matter that he had allowed a child-killer to escape, possibly to kill again.

The jury, it seemed, also did not believe the story told by David Burgess. They took just three hours and twenty minutes to decide, unanimously, that Burgess was guilty of both murders. He was then sentenced to life imprisonment. As he was led down to the cells, David Burgess had a broad smile on his face. As for the murder of Yolande Waddington, Burgess was never linked to that crime and it remains, to this day, an unsolved murder.

CHAPTER 15

The Elvis Fan
Barbara Frances Browne
1966–67

Roy Browne first met Barbara, the woman who would become his wife, in 1942, when she was just fourteen years old. A relationship developed and, in 1948, when she was twenty, they married. A daughter, Roylene was soon born to the union and to all intents, Roy and Barbara were happy enough together. Things changed, however, in 1959 when Barbara Browne suffered a miscarriage. Ever since that time, she had been moody and depressed.

Indeed, one might almost say, she retreated into her own childhood for her behaviour became rather strange. She began to collect dolls and built a sort of shrine to them. One day, Roy even found one of the dolls carefully positioned on top of the wardrobe. One might think that this was not an undue cause for concern, but Barbara had given this doll the name Carla, the same name she had selected for the daughter she miscarried.

Still, Barbara had one great interest, which Roy encouraged. After all, it took her mind off things and made her happy. Roy, therfore, had no concerns whatsoever when Barbara founded an Elvis Presley Fan Club which met, on a regular basis at Watlington House, in Watlington Street, Reading.

By all accounts, the club was a success and Barbara soon

managed to recruit many new members. Two of those members were Peter Whittaker and Sheila Griffin, who both joined around June 1965. These two youngsters seemed to get on very well together and in due course, Peter asked Sheila out. She agreed, and the relationship between the two blossomed. Finally, they discussed marriage and it was agreed that they would become officially engaged on Sheila's twenty-first birthday, 7 February 1967.

That, however, was in the future. For now, Peter continued to live at 108 Crockhamwell Road, Woodley and drive around on his motorbike, whilst Sheila lived at Amherst Road, Reading and caught the bus to her work for the Automobile Association.

In fact, Peter had known the Browne family ever since he was a child. They lived at 18 Silver Fox Crescent, also in Woodley and he had grown up with their daughter, Roylene. They had played together as children and he had been to Barbara Browne's house many times. It was no real surprise then, when in September 1966, Barbara offered Peter a lift home when his motorbike broke down. That journey back to Woodley would prove to be very fateful indeed.

As Barbara drove Peter home, they talked about his relationship with Sheila and the discussion they had had about getting married. Barbara made the comment that she didn't think Sheila was good enough for him. That might well have surprised Peter, but what came next shocked him far more, for Barbara confessed she was in love with him.

The fact that she was forty years old, whilst he was half that age, or that she was married and he was about to become engaged, did not seem to dissuade Barbara. They talked further and the drive to Woodley became a detour to a wood just outside Reading where the couple had sex for the first time.

Despite her apparent disapproval of Sheila Griffin, Barbara had also been known, occasionally, to give her lifts too. On 7 December 1966, Barbara gave Sheila a lift home from the offices of the Automobile Association. Exactly one week later, on 14

Bulmershe Road, on the left of the map, where Barbara Browne killed Sheila Griffin. Author's Collection

December, she did the same again, but this time, Sheila was never to complete her journey.

We will never know what words passed between Barbara Browne and Sheila Griffin in that car on 14 December 1966 but we do know that Barbara drove to Bulmershe Road, where she threw ammonia into Sheila's face. She then picked up a copper-headed mallet, which she had secreted by the driver's seat, and struck Sheila over the head at least twenty-one times. Satisfied that the young girl was dead, Barbara then placed a plastic bag over her head, which she tied in place with a stocking. She then used a scarf to wipe the blood off the windscreen before driving home to 18 Silver Fox Crescent.

At the time Barbara arrived home, Roy Browne was in a workshop he had built for himself in the attic. He heard Barbara drive up to the house and put the car into the garage. Then he heard her call for him to come down, adding that she had just done something terrible.

When Roy Browne saw his wife, it was clear that something terrible had indeed happened. Her face and clothing were covered in blood but before he could ask her what had happened, Barbara said that she had just killed someone and wanted his help in disposing of the body. Calmly, Roy suggested that she should go and wash the blood from her face. Barbara did as he suggested and whilst she was cleaning herself, Roy went to the garage to check on the car. There he saw the body of Sheila Griffin, still in the front passenger seat. Knowing what he had to do next, Roy locked the garage doors and went to telephone for the police.

Constable Derek Gardiner timed his arrival at Silver Fox Crescent at 7.15pm. He too checked on the scene inside the car and then went to interview Barbara Browne. She made no attempt to avoid the consequences of what she had done, saying: 'I killed her. She is in the van. Take me. Where are your handcuffs?'

Constable Gardiner cautioned Barbara but she continued to speak adding: 'I killed her. I do not know why I killed her. Oh God what a merry Christmas this will be. I killed her. I hit her, and hit her, and hit her. She was a wicked girl.'

Although Barbara appeared to be much calmer than when she had first arrived home, it was still thought best to call out a doctor to examine her. Doctor William G Cheyne saw Barbara at her home and began by asking her how she was feeling now. Barbara merely replied: 'I have just killed someone.' Dr Cheyne made his examination and determined that Barbara was suffering from depression.

Charged with murder, Barbara Browne's final committal hearing took place before the magistrates on Wednesday 31 January 1967, after which she was sent to face her trial at Oxford in February. She duly appeared before Mr Justice Chapman on 27 February, where she pleaded not guilty to murder but guilty to manslaughter. That plea was not accepted by the prosecution, who stated they wished to proceed on the charge of murder. After some discussion, it was ruled that the case should be put back to the next Berkshire Assizes where the evidence would be heard.

Barbara Browne finally appeared at Reading on 24 April before Mr Justice Howard. The case for the prosecution was detailed by Mr Charles Lawson whilst Barbara's defence rested in the hands of Mr Douglas Draycott.

In effect, since Barbara had admitted being responsible for Sheila's death, the only case to hear was concerning her mental state at the time. For this reason, many of those who would normally have appeared in court to give their testimony, instead had their statements read out to the court.

Constable Gardiner detailed the various statements Barbara had made to him, both before and after he had cautioned her. His testimony was followed by the reading out of a statement made by the dead girl's father, Mr Wallace Griffin.

In this, Mr Griffin said that his daughter had worked for the Automobile Association for some four years. She had been going to the Elvis fan club for almost two years and it was there that she met Peter Whittaker. They started seeing each other in May 1966 and had arranged to become engaged on 7 February.

Peter Whittaker's statement referred to his relationship with Barbara Browne and claimed that his girlfriend knew about the relationship. He said that Sheila had not objected because they felt they were not ready for a sexual relationship yet and this was a way for Peter to satisfy his needs without risking Sheila becoming pregnant.

Doctor Peter Scott had made a psychiatric examination of the defendant and determined that she was of at least average intelligence. She was not suffering from any psychiatric illness, but was certainly childish and emotionally shallow. She had become obsessed with Peter Whittaker and had started to collect souvenirs of him. Thus, she had saved a number of stubs from cigarettes, which he had smoked, and some cups he had drunk from. She had also kept a condom used by him on one of their sexual liaisons.

After Roy Browne had given his testimony, Doctor Edmund O'Connell, the family doctor, was called. He detailed a history of depression going back to 1959, after her miscarriage. He too had been called to the Browne house after Barbara's arrest and said that he had found her completely devoid of any emotion.

The final witness was Doctor Bertram Mantelbrote of the Littlemore Hospital, who testified that Barbara showed evidence of a personality disorder of a persistent kind. He detailed examples of this, including the fact that Barbara had been in the habit of writing to her own teddy bear. She would write the bear a letter using her left hand and then reply to herself, as the bear, with her right.

After a trial lasting four days, the jury of nine men and three women took just seven minutes to decide that Barbara Browne was not responsible for her actions and thus, was guilty of manslaughter, not murder. The judge ruled that she should be sent to the Fairmile Hospital for treatment.

CHAPTER 16

Sacrifice
Olton Goring and Eileen Goring
1971

The neighbours had had enough. For the best part of a week now, there had been chanting and shouting from the house at 19 Waylen Street, Reading and this had culminated on the night of Tuesday 19 January 1971 with stamping, the sound of girls screaming and wailing, and still more chanting. It was time to call in the police.

The police did indeed attend, but they failed to quieten the racket coming from the house. They had determined that the occupants of the house, Olton Goring, his wife Eileen and their children, were all members of a fundamentalist sect, but even when officers called in a pastor from the church, the noise still continued. The neighbours were spoken to and they reported that in addition to the noise, there had also been a naked woman hanging out of an upstairs window and spitting into the street below.

It seemed that the only way out might be some sort of civil action in the courts.

The noise, already intolerable, increased even further over the night of 25 January and it soon became clear that something more than a religious chanting was going on at number 19. So awful did things become that on Wednesday 27 January, neighbours broke into the house and tried to quieten things down for themselves. What they found caused the police to be called for again. This time, officers could take direct action for, on the landing, they found the body of sixteen-year-old Keith Anderson Goring, one of the sons of Olton and Eileen.

Taken into custody, Olton and Eileen made various appearances before the magistrates where Mr Rodney Higgins, for the prosecution, opposed bail for both of the accused. They were, consequently, remanded in custody having been advised to seek legal aid.

The inquest on the dead boy was opened on Tuesday 2 February before the Deputy Coroner of Reading, Mr Arthur Sheppard. Evidence of identity was given by Brenda Rowen Goring, the dead boy's sister, who said that Keith had been born on 21 March 1952, in Barbados. He was a labourer who had wanted to join the army when he was old enough.

Medical evidence was given by Dr Arthur Keith Mant, a pathologist from Harley Street, who told the court that he had first seen the body at 2.00am on 27 January. At a subsequent post-mortem, Dr Mant had determined that Keith Goring had died from asphyxia as a result of compression to his neck. There were signs of manual compression and there was no possibility of it being self-inflicted. The inquest was then adjourned so that the police might make further inquiries.

The final appearance before the magistrates took place on 3 March when both defendants were committed for trial at the next Oxford Assizes. When that trial finally took place, before Mr Justice Milmo, Mr O B Popplewell and Mr JP Smith appeared for the Director of Public Prosecutions. Mr John Marchie appeared for Olton Goring whilst Mr Nicholas Freeman appeared for Eileen. She pleaded not guilty to murder whilst her husband pleaded guilty but with diminished responsibility.

There could be little doubt that Olton and Eileen were responsible for the death of their son. In addition to their own statements to the police, there had also been statements from some of the Goring's other children and these allowed the authorities to build up a picture of what had taken place inside 19 Waylen Street.

Apparently, the entire family had engaged in a week of fasting and chanting in the belief that this would render them into a state of religious meditation. During the state of trance thus induced, it was believed that members of the sect would be possessed by the Holy Spirit, and be able to talk in tongues.

On Saturday 23 January, Keith had been seen hanging out of the window, waving his arms about and coughing violently. This was not, however, some attempt at seeking help or assistance for there was also the incident of the naked woman spitting into the street and the fact that one of Keith's sisters had been made to cough repeatedly for a long period of time. This, it transpired, was a way to get rid of demons.

In due course, some of the children were sent to stay with friends in Reading. Soon after this, Olton Goring told the remainder of his family that one of them would soon be killed by a destroying angel.

At around midnight on the night he died, Keith, along with the other remaining members of his family, went into his mother's room. They found Eileen Goring in a frenzied state and Olton then announced that Keith would have to be sacrificed in order to save his mother's life.

The other sons of the family were then ordered to sit on Keith whilst Eileen and Olton beat him. Once this was done, Olton then held Keith down whilst Eileen walked up and down his body. Finally, Olton strangled his son whilst his wife looked on. When the police finally arrived at the premises soon afterwards, Olton had shouted to them: 'Glory, glory. Give me strength.'

With so much evidence against them, the defence teams did not dispute the basic facts but sought to show that both defendants had been suffering from some mental instability at the time they killed their son.

Doctor Paul Doran was the medical officer at Holloway prison where Eileen Goring had been held. He had interviewed Eileen, who told him that she had been deeply concerned about her son's attitude to their religion since the beginning of the year. She went on to say that the family were members of the Pentecostal Church and had participated in the chanting, fasting and dancing as part of their religious faith.

On 19 January, Eileen had seen her family doctor, complaining of feeling physically unwell and rather depressed. Since her admission to prison, this had not really improved and she seemed to be exhausted. In Dr Doran's opinion, Eileen was suffering from a severe mental illness at the time she had taken part in the attack upon her son.

This testimony was confirmed by that of Dr David Duncan, who had also examined Eileen and testified that at the time of the murder she would not have known the nature and quality of her actions.

After listening to all the medical evidence, the trial judge directed the jury to find Eileen Goring guilty by reason of insanity. Olton, of course, had already entered a plea of guilty with diminished responsibility and it remained only to sentence them both.

Orton Goring was sentenced to be confined in Broadmoor, for an unlimited period. His wife, Eileen, was ordered to undergo a regime of treatment in hospital. No other prosecutions followed from the tragic death of Keith Goring.

Index